Hippolyte Taine

Journeys Through France

Being Impressions of the Provinces

Hippolyte Taine

Journeys Through France
Being Impressions of the Provinces

ISBN/EAN: 9783744744041

Printed in Europe, USA, Canada, Australia, Japan

Cover: Foto ©Andreas Hilbeck / pixelio.de

More available books at **www.hansebooks.com**

TAINE'S WORKS.

Uniform edition, 12mo, green cloth,

TRAVELLING IN SOUTHERN FRANCE. 12mo.	$2 50
ITALY (Rome and Naples).	2 50
ITALY (Florence and Venice).	2 50
NOTES ON ENGLAND. With Portrait.	2 50
A TOUR THROUGH THE PYRENEES.	2 50
NOTES ON PARIS.	2 50
HISTORY OF ENGLISH LITERATURE. 2 vols.	5 00
ON INTELLIGENCE. 2 vols.	5 00
LECTURES ON ART. First Series. Containing The Philosophy of Art; The Ideal in Art.	2 50
LECTURES ON ART. Second Series. Containing The Philosophy of Art in Italy; The Philosophy of Art in the Netherlands; The Philosophy of Art in Greece.	2 50
THE ANCIENT RÉGIME.	2 50
THE FRENCH REVOLUTION. 3 vols.	7 50
THE MODERN RÉGIME. 2 vols.	5 00

SEPARATE EDITIONS.

ENGLISH LITERATURE. 4 vols. With 28 portraits on wood. Large 12mo.	
The same from other plates. 12mo.	1 25
ENGLISH LITERATURE condensed by Fiske. 1 vol. Large 12mo. *net,*	1 40
A TOUR THROUGH THE PYRENEES. With illustrations by Gustave Doré. 8vo.	10 00
Full levant morocco.	20 00
LES ORIGINES DE LA FRANCE CONTEMPORAINE. Extracts with English Notes. 16mo. Boards. *net.*	50

HENRY HOLT & CO., PUBLISHERS,
NEW YORK.

JOURNEYS THROUGH FRANCE

BEING

IMPRESSIONS OF THE PROVINCES

BY

H. A. TAINE, D.C.L.

With Seven Illustrations

NEW YORK
HENRY HOLT AND COMPANY
1897

CONTENTS.

PART I.

	PAGE
Douai	1
Le Mans	14
La Flèche	20
Solesmes	26
From Le Mans to Rennes	33
Rennes	35
The Museum at Rennes	40
From Rennes to Le Mans and Tours	54
Bordeaux	60
From Bordeaux to Toulouse	66
Toulouse	68
Strolls in Toulouse	69
From Toulouse to Cette	85
Cette	87
From Cette to Marseilles	92
Marseilles	96
From Marseilles to Lyons	107
From Lyons to Besançon	117
Besançon	119
From Besançon to Strasbourg	127
Strasbourg	129

CONTENTS.

PART II.

	PAGE
DOUAI	135
AMIENS	138
AN EXCURSION TO ST. MALO	140
POITIERS	142
ARCACHON	154
TOULOUSE	162
MONTPELLIER	166
MARSEILLES	171
PROVENCE	179
BOURG EN BRESSE	182
BESANÇON	186
NANCY	189
RHEIMS	196

PART III.

DOUAI	205
LA FLÈCHE	211
FROM RENNES TO REDON	214
VANNES	217
FROM AURAY TO CARNAC	225
THE CATHEDRAL OF NANTES	232
FROM NANTES TO ANGERS	234
THE PICTURE-GALLERY AT ANGERS	235
TOULOUSE	238
CARCASSONNE	247
CETTE	252
A VISIT TO AIGUES-MORTES	255
FROM ARLES TO MARSEILLES	259
BERRE	270
ORANGE	276
LYONS	280
CROSSING THE JURA	283
STRASBOURG	285

JOURNEYS THROUGH FRANCE.

DOUAI.

August 20, 1863.—Here are some of the impressions borne in upon me during an after-dinner walk.

Over all there is a distinct sense of comfort, not unlike what one feels in Flanders and in England. Nowhere is one reminded of the petty respectability of the midland towns, with their fussing and over-reaching activity.

Before I left Paris I had witnessed the illuminations of August 15, the crowds in the squares and dusty streets, the white walls, the eager and contorted faces, the sight-seers, domestic servants and working-men, gathered together for their draught of miscalled pleasure, which cheated them like a cup of adulterated cocoa. I had absorbed the all-pervading odour, the dust and steam of life, the inferno of feverish hurry, the plague of unsatisfied cupidity. But here I found less heat; and on the following day there was rain. The brick-built, steep-roofed houses, in the style of

Louis XIII., have solid and lofty chimneys, and vaulted windows with leaden lattice and small panes of glass. Nothing was casual, nothing for mere show, but all for lasting enjoyment.

There were a few people walking in the streets; a hum of life was just audible; here and there I saw a tradesman in his shop, or a woman reading or gazing about her, dressed in her Sunday frock. She was quite content to adorn herself and rest. Everything was clean, and there were frequent signs of good taste; everywhere space and elbow-room, and no hint of over-crowding. Many houses have something to attract you in their fronts or in their roofs, such as you never see in the regulated monotony of the Rue de Rivoli. These folk may be half asleep, but they are "warm," and their great-grandfathers were artists. The Scarpe meanders through the town, and creates many a miniature Venice. There were ducks paddling about at their ease; an old lady was watching them from her window, as she sat amongst her flowers. It was a Sunday evening picture.

These high rooms and venerable houses present much that is picturesque. Some are reached by steps from the water below; some rise sheer from the canal, which winds about them in curious sort, reflecting their bright red tiles; now and then they are severed by a fringe of garden, and we are refreshed by the sight of a tree.

Next day, as I said, there was rain, and at once we had the familiar north-country landscape, with its wan or dissolving mists, snow-white or black as soot, rolling over the red roofs and the masses of green foliage. As soon as the rain has ceased, the indented roof cuts clear into the lightened air, and the eye is gladdened by the honest hues of bright uncompromising red. Seen from the ramparts, a score of subjects for Flemish pictures meet the eye. Every house has a tongue; whereas in Paris you have but business streets, ornamental façades, and lodging-houses.

What pleased me most was the Scarpe, as it passed through the town like a broad canal. Fresh water always puts new life into me, especially when it flows full between its banks, and is green, and ripples with little waves. The glazed walls, the pretty painted houses, capriciously and irregularly built, glimmer in the water, and put on a new charm of brightness and gaiety. Very welcome to me, fresh from the dust of Paris, was this long clean road, beside the wholesome stream, with scarcely a soul passing by, and in all but complete silence.

Still more to my mind is the Scarpe outside the town. Tufted reeds, the most luxuriant I have ever seen, crowd and jostle each other in the ditches beneath the ramparts; the quiet river curves in and out, with long dark sweeps between the double row of poplars, under the big peaceful boats. The river has been turned into a canal, and its tranquillity earned for it that distinction. As I went indoors the setting sun displayed its beauty, and a pink flush spread itself with exultant joy over all the shadowed green.

Douai is an old Catholic city, once the seat of a Parliament and a University; they used to call it the Athens of the North. More than one wealthy magistrate, living on his estate in arrogance and ease, invite you to excellently-appointed dinners. Ten or a dozen families give balls every winter. There is no mean economy; many keep their carriage, own land, and live in settled comfort. The younger folk attend classes and lectures. I heard of one professor who lectured to two or three hundred in the winter months, and to a hundred in summer.

Here I came across several of my old friends, X. amongst the number. He occupied a house to himself, with a garden, a gate opening on the river, and out-buildings, at a rent of twelve hundred francs. His wife came from Bordeaux, and they married for love. She had begun to lose her health, but recovered it twice as quickly as she might have done when she obtained permission to marry as soon as she was well. She received me in a coloured apron, having come straight from the kitchen. She had all the southern volubility.

"I live my life indoors. My husband scolds me for it, but I tell him that he likes his food well cooked. He wants me to go into society, but I have been nowhere for three years. It fatigues me; and there is so much to do in a house with two children!"

She was in great trouble when they first arrived; the rooms are high, the curtains were too short, and they had to be made all over again.

"Oh, he shall not go to Paris; I put down my foot against that. We should be too uncomfortable there; we are going to stay where we are."

There are many housewives of this kind in the provinces. At table they have not the nerve to say much, and are ill at ease; they do not go into society, because it makes them uncomfortable. One of them I knew who had an income of six thousand francs, and three children; she looked after them with a single nurse, and spent part of the day in the kitchen. My friends tell me that they are all exceedingly domestic, except one or two who lay themselves out to be fashionable, like Parisian ladies. A country wife often finds her sole employment, and the sufficient exercise of her faculties, in needlework, darning, and the management of her household.

Living is cheap, and does not overtax the energies. With six thousand francs a family can be very comfortable. With twice as much, one may keep a horse and a small carriage; many people retire on two or three thousand francs a year.

The official class are conventional and anxious to please; the chief officials, who always wear a white tie, and are constantly bowing and smiling, pour forth a perpetual mechanical stream of compliments; they delight in soothing historical lectures, to which parents are wont to take their daughters. It is a finishing course of education: the lecturer knows how to trip lightly over the muddy patches. Mons. B., who lectures in philosophy, has an audience of barely twenty, and he has been reprimanded by his superiors for saying that the Stoics had a fine system of morality.

There are no serious students or workers. The well-to-do folk come to these public lectures by force of habit, by way of passing an hour. The audience includes magistrates, officers, and retired functionaries. The Faculty is a literary restaurant, a kind of intellectual Petite Provence, whither you may come when the fire of life is gently cooling on its ashes.

The College is large and fine, spacious, healthy and well arranged, sheltered by trees, and with broad courts; but the students always present that poor and shamefaced appearance which is produced by the constrained life of the cloister. I also visited the English College, which sent Catholic missionaries and martyrs to England. It is enormous, like the other, but its students' rooms are on a paltry scale, reminding me of the old and dirty desks at which we used to sit. It was the same with the dormitories. There is a new chapel; the ancient fresco and the rest of the interior were destroyed in 1789. A few pictures and portraits remain, amongst them one of Cardinal Allen, with a pale, wasted and shrunken face, and a fine white beard, like that of Richelieu. There were also the grave and honest heads, strong and narrow, of martyrs and doctors belonging to the sixteenth and seventeenth centuries. All the brothers are English, and so are the pupils, with the exception of seven or eight French boys. There is a good library, in which I noticed Erasmus and Voltaire.

These great establishments, like the Abbey of Senone, suggest to us the picture of a life full of dulness, of settled calm and serenity, the sort of life which overtakes a corporation, a community of monks, hard-working men of all kinds who pursue their labour under calm and unselfish conditions, so different from our ordinary individualism and fever.

Clerical influence is here very strong, especially on the wealthier classes. "What should we come to if it were not for religion?" they ask. And in fact the clergy are a vast intellectual police. Their influence on the masses is also great. The curé pays his visit to his flock whilst the husband is at work.

"And so, my good woman, you want to see the destruction of our holy religion, and the ruin of the Holy Father himself?"

"Oh, your reverence!" (Monsieur le Doyen.)

"Well, then, why are you going to vote for So-and-so?"

"Dame! Because the mayor gave us the ticket!"

"It is a bad ticket."

"Oh, if it is a bad one, please take it away, your reverence, and give us another. I am sure I don't want to see our holy religion destroyed, and I will see that my husband votes with your ticket."

And the husband votes accordingly.

The peasants of the neighbourhood, and the workmen, are docile and sensible; they keep steadily at work, and are easily managed. Not so the Picardy men, who are apt, if they fall out with their master, to turn on him with a knife. But these, though they are essentially Flemings, talk very lightly of the Flemish folk, and regard themselves as genuine "Franchais." They have a natural bent for co-operation; they have their musical societies, cross-bow and archery clubs, and so forth; and they have sufficient perseverance to learn all these things. They are naturally coarse; they drink hard, and the women are easy and over-generous in their moods, as their husbands usually have cause to know before marrying. But the neighbours quite expect that a promise to marry shall be kept, and that the first child shall be born in wedlock.

I met plenty of true Flemish faces in the streets, with large noses, hollow cheeks, prominent jaws and cheek-bones, the complexion of a potato, red hair and light eyes. One or two of the girls were as buxom as any painted by Rubens.

There are a few relics of the earlier occupations of the country, amongst them a half-Flemish, half-Spanish belfry, square-built, with four little round towers clinging to the corners, and an extraordinary Chinese cap of leaden baubles and cupolas stuck on above, with a lion to surmount the whole. There is also a museum of curiosities collected by Dr Escalier, who is by no means well off, containing a few second-rate Flemish pictures and drawings, a group of skaters sufficiently true to life, and a fine study of a woman's back. At Ste. Marie's there is a "Sainteté," by one of Heneling's pupils, weak enough by the side of his master; but it displays the same feeling of mystic resignation. The town museum is a remarkable jumble of modern affectation, copies and odds and ends from various schools, with one good portrait of Van Dyck's time, and a few tolerably authentic Flemish pictures, the dispersions of a main stream which found its channel elsewhere.

I paid a visit to a sugar-factory. This is in a flat and marshy district, so that it has been necessary to dig canals in order to let the water off. These are veritably Low Countries, and that implies everything, morally and physically. There is no slope in the land, a great deal of marsh remains, and here and there you may see, amongst the fields of beet-root and wheat, broad pools, motionless and glistening, with borders of rustling tufted reeds.

Two days' rain has left the land water-logged. The soil could not receive it all; the Scarpe has overflowed, and will have to discharge its burden at some distance below the dykes. If the town was gloomy this morning, so is the country. The rain is excessive; it streams down through the liquid, murky sky till everything drips and oozes; the horizon has disappeared; our feet splash up the mud. There are, withal, intermittent gleams of delightful sunshine, when the rain is gilded by rays straightway extinguished by the falling mist;

the grace as of a woman is displayed by the surrounding verdure, cheered as it weeps.

There is landscape everywhere. From the windows of the factory and of the house, as from the carriage at every turning of the road, there is a subject ready for the artist — the high-pitched roofs of the houses, the scattered poplars, the low tree-lines on the horizon, the broad open sky, studded with clouds, a group of barefooted children climbing about the trunk of a fallen tree, a cluster of peasants on the bridge. I suppose it is because the country is so well defined in its character; everything stands out and asserts itself.

The workpeople are thoroughly Flemish. They smoke over their work, and driving their carts; their pipes, a good foot in length, hang from their mouths as they fill up their sacks. Half-an-hour every day has to be allowed them for smoking. There they sit, half-stripped, in long rows, puffing at their pipes in the chilly fog. On Sundays they will drink as many as fifteen or sixteen half-pints of beer, with a dash of brandy in it.

All the country-folk have enough land to provide them with a store of potatoes, as well as a horse or a mule, or at any rate a donkey. They work in the factory from September to January; even the well-to-do peasants take their share in this work.

They are punctual, easily managed, handy with the machinery. A machine is best handled by your north-country workman, not by the haphazard plunger of the south.

It is a hard life for the intelligent young manager, whom I found a good fellow, with plenty of determination. All day long he is busy over his vats of molasses, or driving bargains, with no company but that of his workmen, the colour of a turnip, tramping barefoot amidst the machinery, and shut up in the evenings within the four walls of his brick-built house, or in his little garden of some half-dozen paces from hedge to hedge. There is nothing for it in that country but to marry and beget children.

There are no refined enjoyments for the younger members of good families. They betake themselves to the place to which Cato the Elder used to send the youth of Rome. When they are fairly grown up, their fathers grow tired of seeing them about the house, and get them married: a rich and well-connected girl is produced, and the young man suffers himself to be disposed of. They are fairly steady. At the clubs — and that is the worst of them—young fellows take too much. It is natural to the North German, the Fleming, and the Englishman. One of my friends said to me: "In Paris, as soon as work is over, the first thing we think about is how we are going to amuse ourselves. You will only find that in Paris." He is right. In Belgium they marry, and have a family; then comes the second establishment, and so on, from bad to worse. When the Englishman has ceased to work, he eats and drinks, turns red in the face, becomes gloomy or quarrelsome, takes his pleasures brutally, swears and fights. After that he sleeps till he is sober, and in the morning he washes his face in hot water and his body in cold water, brushes up his whiskers, and goes about his business with a funereal aspect. I think it is only the Frenchman, the Latin, the Southerner, who combines art, poetry or refinement with his pleasure. The other is either a mere brute or merely virtuous.

LE MANS.

RETURNING from Douai, one sees on the horizon, in the direction of Arras, a fine-looking tower, probably that of the town hall. In all these Flemish towns, as at Bruges and Brussels, I know that there are masterpieces of metal work in the public buildings. Even the glasses they drink out of are masterpieces. They are artists by their sense of form and colour, as well as by their music.

After Amiens there is a long, uninviting stretch of Picardy, grey and bare. The harvest is over, and there is no tree, no water, nothing but chalky patches. Presently we get back to the climate and soil familiar to the Parisian, a wonderful contrast. I found them near Beauce, on the morning after I had left Douai. There is something refined and charming in the scenery; nothing especially striking, but nooks of verdure, lovely streams, a pleasant diversity of cultivation, and picturesque villages.

LE MANS.
THE HOUSE OF QUEEN BÉRENGÈRE.

Near Le Mans, shortly before you come to it, there is a great change. Here the pastoral country begins; the meadows, as in Normandy, are surrounded by quickset hedges, with many large trees. Thus every meadow is well marked out. The winding roads are lined with thickets, and are lower than the fields, for the winter rains scour them out. These walls of green are delightful in the bright sunlight. After Flanders, it inspires you with new life.

Le Mans is decidedly ugly. There is the same contrast between the country and its inhabitants which I have noticed in all the midland districts. One is charmed by a few relics of other days, such as an avenue of venerable trees, an occasional thick belt of hornbeam by the roadside full of murmuring life, a church with a couple of tiled belfries, grave and simple as a nun. But everywhere there is neglect, incongruity, an absence of anything like attention. It all smacks of the political order of things which plants an administration on a town as a dentist plants a set of teeth on a shrunken gum. The streets and buildings have no character. Plenty of stone here and plaster there; villas for monied nobodies and retired respectabilities, some ornamental, some dilapidated; macadamised roads, followed by other roads laid with rough cobbles; a great unpaved open space, irregular in shape and not even reduced to a level; at one end a horse fair, with a score of indifferent horses being put through their paces; in the middle, two cows awaiting their turn.

You are soon made aware of the presence of energetic and clamorous tradesmen, displaying their novelties from Paris. In the window of a bookshop hangs the portrait of Monsignor X., a round, fresh-faced, spectacled man, full of smiles, like a Chinese jar. That man has dined, dozed with his hands on his belly, pronounced the benediction with nicely disposed fingers, and smiled with a sanctified air at the compliments and effusiveness of his devotees. I saw two or three ladies coming out of a shop, gaily dressed and wearing pretty little bonnets, who threw back their heads like happy peacocks. Dress is the only characteristic of the national genius which I found developed at Le Mans. I also went through the market, a squalid commonplace hole, occupied by paltry stalls, and by the countryfolk who had come in to stock them.

How well one understands, in the course of such a walk as this, the social condition of France! How low the whole nation stands, how little raised above the serfs and burgesses of the Middle Age, with an official class taking the place of the old nobility! This superior official class provides the rest, without so much as being asked, with markets, colleges, law-courts, and all kinds of grandmotherly intervention. In a word, the masses have what they want—the petty life of their towns, and the means of selling their corn and their produce as they think proper.

I have been thinking of all this whilst following my new calling, and, to be brief, if you exclude the natural roguery and rank dishonesty of men in high places, take no account of the Rastignacs, and regard the matter as a whole, this country has reached a high level of justice and prosperity. We practise equality; no favours are shown, even towards the noble and the rich; justice is independent, without respect of persons. The most conspicuous feature, which has produced at once the greatest amount of good and evil, is this: The modern builders of France seem to have argued that there are a certain number of things which are worth having, and that everyone must have his share—no one too large a share, but almost everyone a small or a middling-sized share. Generals of division, bishops, principals, rectors, directors and the like, figure at about fifteen thousand francs. Small places, varying from twelve hundred to three thousand francs, abound. Every income rises a trifle after three or six years; you are to have a rise of a hundred, five hundred, francs, a first or second step in the Legion of Honour. Even in their old age the masses are looked after, in asylums or by widows' pensions. There is a gradual move up so long as one lives; everybody can tell more or less certainly how he will stand in twenty years; great and flagrant injustice is all but impossible. There is abundance of petty trouble, discontent, envy, expectation, spending and saving, but no overwhelming despair. It is an ordered existence; everyone pinches himself, and grumbles, and waits for his rise.

The professor of applied mathematics in this town has an income of four thousand francs. He began on eighteen hundred, giving eight lectures a week, and in ten years he rose to his four thousand. He consoles himself with the honour of the position; he is a unit in the system; he is unwilling to sacrifice his past, and lives in hope of some small promotion. There are peevish individuals here and there, or men who think themselves ill-used, like the lieutenant who teaches swimming, fencing and gymnastics; but they cannot expect to shatter the enormous machine which is but France herself. In short, you must have your prepossession in statecraft, as well as in art. This is one of the desirable things in life, even if it be only half desirable: to suppress the lives of the great, the vested interests, and every kind of heredity and aristocracy; to share and share alike; to manufacture a vast amount of medium culture and medium prosperity; to create fifteen or twenty millions of people who are tolerably happy, to protect them, to restrain them, to bring them under discipline, and, if necessary, to hurl them at an enemy.

LA FLÈCHE.

AFTER leaving Le Mans the country is delightful. I came from Noyen to La Flèche on the outside of the diligence, through clustering verdure of many different kinds, under wide-spreading trees, in the stillness and calm of evening. The Touraine landscapes begin at this point on the Loir, with their voluptuous glamour, with the warm, caressing climate which the Valois princes used to love, with the peaceful rivers gliding gently over their sands, lying broad from bank to bank and slumbering between grassy slopes—all but the eddies and rapids of the back water. The river widens out towards the bridge, close to a high mill which presents the appearance of a tower, and glistens like a sheet of ice under the placid sun. Straight in front of me, on the wide, green, level plain, the light foliage quivers, and the poplars rustle their few remaining leaves. The azure sky is flushed with brightness; the air is flecked with diamonds between the slender branches; the verdure clothes

LA FLÈCHE ON THE LOIR.

itself in softer tints, for, though nourished by the stream, the sun has touched it into brown or gold. The eyes are at rest amid this deeper colouring; there comes a sense of joy as they sweep the radiant surface of the water, and life once more seems gracious and kind.

At La Flèche the landscape in itself is of a Flemish type, though the sky differs. There is in both cases the river meandering across a low-lying level plain, and dotted with islands; the same meadow-land, the same hedges with their occasional poplars; and in both the floods are out in the winter. But the sun changes everything. Under its rays all is calm and joyous allurement. The clear water heaves in answer to the sky, and ripples in a lattice-work of wonderful azure—bright, luminous blue, framed in tender green, with cloudlets of swansdown above. The streams of a level country run continuous with the land, making no banks to speak of. The sky fills a wide vault of heaven, and it seems to me to possess the true southern luminosity, with all its velvet brilliance. It makes you think of lapis lazuli, and many a glowing gem.

I spent part of two evenings seated on a beam of wood opposite to the landing-stage. Here the river occupies a wide, stone-edged lock basin, with a little flood-gate which keeps up a constant murmur. Two or three high buildings stand in the middle of the basin, and are used as tanneries.

I cannot convey an adequate idea of the beauty, the calm, the delightful softness of the scene; that would need the pencil of a Decamps or a Corot. The clear sky shines out above like the pearly lining of a shell, the broad sheet of water reflects its light, and the upper and the under glow meet and float impalpably in the delicate breath of the mist. This transparent veil of air softens every outline; the slim trees and the distant poplars seem to be turned to vapour. They might be happy shades floating between existence and extinction, softly, yearningly, as ready to vanish as to reappear. There is no colour; the high buildings throw black shadows over the water, but beyond them the white light flows and shimmers, and the tiny waves rustle in their sport or sink to rest.

La Flèche is a place of eight or ten thousand inhabitants. It is roughly paved with narrow streets, planned after the true type of a country town—on one side a fine modern street, on the other a poverty-stricken quarter, with one-storey houses such as are common in England. A house, large enough for a family, together with a garden, can be had for three hundred francs a year.

The chief ornament of the town is the Prytanée.

There are four hundred pupils, all exhibitioners except twenty, with a general-in-command and his staff. The buildings and gardens cover four hectares. This is the old Jesuits' College founded by Henri IV., and it is quite on a grand scale. In the sixteenth century people demanded more space for breathing and movement than we do. It is an enormous rectangular building enclosing a large grass-covered quadrangle, and to the right and left are many courts and accessory buildings. At the back is a large park, with plantations and flowers, a green stone basin and a fountain, a wood of well-grown timber, and great dykes, like those which surround a castle. Stone, space, trees, were all lavished on this establishment. Labour and land cost little in those days. These immense courts, those high, symmetrical buildings, that grand arched promenade, the church with its high tower and pointed apse, charm the eye as you approach them from the town. It is all noble and spacious in contrast with the petty bourgeois life that is lived amongst the stunted and crowded rows of dwelling-houses. I have been accused of being an aristocrat; and at any rate I think it would be hateful to have to live without such grand and beautiful possessions as the Prytanée.

There is a fine, or very nearly a fine, picture in the church, the subject of which is the Maccabees. There are no images or figures in plaster. The nave is high and the style is that of the Jesuits, with garlands and ribboned consoles; but here this affected style appears fine by contrast.

It might be supposed that all would be peace within—as happy as a Flemish interior. Seen close, it is like a glass of water under a microscope, full of frightful animalcules devouring each other. I met a man who came here when he was quite young. He has bought a garden with a little two-roomed house in the workmen's quarter, and he lives there like the Fontainebleau artists, with his wife and child. He had rooms in the Prytanée, and left because it was too much trouble to keep himself dressed.

"You meet nothing but crinolines and new dresses in the park."

Self-adornment and the latest fashion seem to turn the heads of all the women. Their husbands have incomes of eighteen hundred or two thousand francs; some of three thousand five hundred. There is only one who has four thousand. They must cut down the beef and soup to provide these ribbons. The heads of the old professors are a sight to be seen. But we must bear in mind the poverty of the universities. In most cases these heads would be less peculiar if they had not weathered a storm of misfortunes.

A curious feature, conspicuous amidst the general dulness of provincial life, is the dulness of these pupils themselves. They are gloomy; they appear to be almost destitute of feeling, and cannot even brighten up at table. The friend whom I have mentioned spoke to me of a new arrival from Paris, who lost his head, and excused himself by saying:

"I can't make it out, but I don't know what I am doing to-day."

He stood on his defence, even whilst he displayed his modesty in the presence of his companions. For in Paris self-respect acts as a stimulus.

SOLESMES.

FROM La Flèche I went on to Sablé, and, as it was raining, I took a private carriage. The country looked very green. I have always been struck by the appearance of trees when the rain is falling; they are so full of life and verdure.

From Sablé I proceeded to Solesmes, in order to visit the Benedictine Abbey. Some of the brethren are learned, like Dom Guéranger, a friend of M. Veuillot's. My guide informed me that he is at work on the saints of Anjou, and on the antiquities of Le Mans. Their library is not a very good one, but they have the Abbé Migne's edition of the Fathers. Perhaps five or six out of the sixty are occupied in work.

It is a very attractive building, which might be the mansion of a man with thirty thousand pounds a year. It stands about fifty feet above the bank of the Sarthe, with a walled terrace, a broad walk sheltered by a close hedge on the left, lovely flowers, vines, Chinese glycine plants creeping over the walls, and a fine fig-tree. There is every sign of good taste, pretty designs and lawns. On the right you get an admirable view. The Sarthe winds and disappears behind groups of trees, where the green plain is lost in the horizon. The monks have built a quaint-looking high tower, of several storeys, surmounted by battlements, where they entertain their guests. I was told that they constructed it in 1848, to give work to the labourers. A short time ago they made room here for two-and-twenty guests. The brother, who showed me round, had the manners of one who had mixed in society. He begged that I would do them the honour of sharing their meal. The fact is that they are not ascetic.

He took me to the broad walk, passing under lime-washed stone arches, and winding round a dense thicket. We met the Fathers occasionally. Most of them were reading, and some were well-built men, but thin and pale. There was no cant about them. I had only one greeting which gave me a shock, and that was from a group of novices on the road.

The refectory is panelled with dark wood. A copper lamp hangs in the centre; and through the open windows we looked out on a charming landscape. They drank cider and wine. Their taste, their comfort, and their studious life, reminded me of the ancient abbey near Senones. Indeed, this mode of life is quite as endurable as that of a soldier or a sailor; discipline and custom are all that a man needs. They imply a restricted society, subject to authority, in a fixed home, with every hour accounted for; and the meditative soul has its vista which ends in God.

The abbey looks very well as you approach it, with its tall belfry, round and grey. But the main interest is in the chapel. It is a narrow chapel, built with a crypt. Entering by the west door, I noticed, first of all, the choir with its blazoned windows and dark wooden panelling. Several monks were in their stalls, absorbed in reading. There were a few stiff heads in stone, of the time of Louis XI., approximating towards expression.

The body of the church is characterized by a grand sculptural effect, right and left of the nave. It is very fine and ancient work, said to have been executed by Italian artists, begun, if we accept the dates on the mouldings, in 1496, and finished in 1553. The figures are life-size. On the right is Christ in the Tomb. Mediæval feeling subsists here almost without modification. The ogive, the little arches meeting in a sheaf, the denticulation, the grotesques, a devil, a jester carved in the margin of the piece, fix its epoch with sufficient accuracy.

The Renaissance was but just beginning; really fine work is still almost unknown. The figures are realistic, taken from the life; the artist is still servile; but how closely he has observed nature, and how well he knows her!

On the left is the Entombment of the Virgin. It is a work of admirable piety and calm. The hands are meekly crossed, but you can see that they partly droop—the body is not yet stiff. It is covered with a white shroud, raised at either end by one of the mourners. There is the same idea in the opposite group in regard to the Christ. The other figures, men and women, whether upright or stooped, are disposed round this focus. The work is still too literal, detailed, and stiff; the figures look too short; they strike one as though they were crowded into a cave. But already we have fine heads, full of energy and nobility; and how profoundly tender is the heart which bespeaks itself in the expression and pose of the Virgin!

There are three other subjects, with many figures. The whole effect is monumental: columns, niches, decorative architecture, all indications of the Renaissance. In front of the window, the head of the woman who plants her feet upon the dragon is charming. But what struck me most was the Virgin and S. Joseph, discovering Jesus amongst the doctors.

The S. Joseph is a fine, vigorous Italian peasant; the Virgin is a pretty but firm-looking girl. It is an attractive couple, and the attitudes are well caught and expressed. The Jesus is too fat, with puffed-out cheeks.

This sincerity of art still untaught by rule and convention, copying the truth as it sees it, is altogether pleasing. These men discovered everything for themselves; they were thoroughly alive. It may have been a family, or something in the nature of a complete school, which here expressed and deposited all that it thought and all that it felt. The Doctors, robed in the fashion of the sixteenth century, are true as the heads of Albert Dürer, but also finer. They are said to be portraits of contemporary heretics. One choleric and sanguine figure might well be meant for Luther. All are actual types, audaciously copied and elaborated. This realism astonishes and shocks one a little in sculpture, but in the end it delights one. I specially remember the scandalized, half-angry expression of the first Doctor, a man of substance and energy, who stands in the foreground with a book in his hand.

Again there is a bas-relief, the Massacre of the Innocents. The mother concealing her infant with her arms is a copy from Raphael, but more massive, almost brutally massive.

In this chapel we have a complete picture of the dawn of Art.

I have come across a considerable number of peasants and townsfolk, at Le Mans, Noyen, Sablé, and other places. They only deepen my impression that France is organised on behalf of these classes; and it is a melancholy result.

A community is like a large garden: it is planned for peaches and oranges, or for carrots and cabbages. Our garden is planned entirely for cabbages and carrots. The ideal is that a peasant may eat meat, and that my shoemaker, having made up his pile to three thousand francs a year, may send his son to the Law School. But men who distinguish themselves never rise to eminence. The utmost that they get is a cross, a modest competence; their income just prevents them from starving. Colonel L., who entered the Polytechnic at sixteen, and left it second on the list, has served forty-four years, and has a pension of four thousand francs. Imagine such a case in England!

Thus everything is transient; you can build no superstructure, you cannot establish your family. Moreover, it is all a matter of competition; we are developing the system of the Chinese. We prepare for examinations, we pass examinations, and we fall into line. This system implies a mechanical or a forced education, college life, the high stool from morning to night, boredom, suspense, intrigue, narrow ideas, the spirit of a hireling.

And the competition is necessary. In what other way could we select our candidates? It does not follow that all they are required to learn is indispensable, or even useful in their future career; but it is a test, and removes the suspicion of unfairness. Genuine and disinterested study is precluded. Boys are crammed at preparatory schools, and trained to become candidates and bachelors. At the final history examination, one candidate wrote out the ancient and modern history of a hundred and fifty islands in the Mediterranean; another, twelve pages on the Council of Florence, quoting the Latin witticisms of his period. This prodigy of a candidate was still no more than a sixth-rate man. Such are the fruits of competition: mediocrities and monstrosities.

They have just set up a new competition for telegraphists. You cannot select them without it; and there is plenty of grumbling already!

FROM LE MANS TO RENNES.

I HAVE seen nothing that is grand, but this is one of the most delightful districts through which I have passed.

It is green from first to last. There is scarcely any corn, and only two or three fields of buckwheat; all the rest is laid down in pasture, every meadow being surrounded by a broad, quickset hedge, with many oak trees. These oaks are fed by the constant rain. It rains at Rennes every other day. As far as the eye can reach there is always the same spectacle of little green undulating tracts, with clumps of oaks, full of fresh life, with bright and lustrous foliage which gladdens the eye as a clear musical sound gladdens the ear. Now and then the soil is clayey, and holds the rain. Then belts of green, unspeakably brilliant, furrow the meadow with emerald hues, and patches of still water gleam amongst the reeds and horsetail. Here and there a pool, stirred by the wind, breaks into innumerable ripples. The wide sheet of black and brown, with its quiet undulation, is a strange and extraordinary picture; a sea-gull flits slowly over it, propelled by its great hooked wings.

Throughout my journey the big water-logged clouds, black as coal, dragged heavily along, or broke over the green heads of the oak-trees.

RENNES.

HERE I found in the centre of the town fine, wide, notable streets, well paved, and with granite-edged sidewalks; but no evidence of taste. The town was burnt in the eighteenth century. The cathedral, with columns clustered in console fashion, has nothing external which is of interest, whilst the interior is white and flat. It is the ugliest building I have seen.

In some parts of the town, though not in the principal streets or the suburbs, the execrable, sharp-pointed, torturing pavement still subsists—nothing more nor less than stones of every size and shape rammed down together. The houses are wretched, a mere mediæval relic. They are built of wood and mortar, tun-bellied and humped, covered with a sort of cracked breastplate of old rough slates, dirty and insecure. There is every imaginable shape; it is the oddest conceivable medley. Some have pointed fifteenth-century caps, some shoot up into turrets, others are short and squat; they greet you with face or flank, in any and every aspect. All have the little guillotine window, with dirty panes of glass. As a shelter against the rain the highest houses have a sort of protruding screen made of slates, resting on a couple of beams. You catch sight of dark, worm-eaten flights of steps, of evil odour. Here, under rain or heavy clouds, is ample suggestion for a painter.

I found a few traces of dull piety and Catholic reaction, such as a monster cross of bronze on a gilded ball, with a vast granite pedestal, set up in 1817. I also heard an emphatic charge from the bishop on the general degeneracy of character, and on the nobility of the Bretons. These episcopal groans, which hurl thunder at modern civilisation, wind up with a permission to eat eggs.

There is profound faith, intensity, and deep devotion in the kneeling crowd. I saw some women at confession, and one of them, who might have been a housekeeper, was telling her beads. A peasant woman prostrated herself before the great cross in the square. The land is Catholic, not by routine, but with passionate conviction. I went to-day to see the congregation disperse after mass and vespers. Some of the older peasants were kneeling on the pavement, with rosaries in their hands, telling their beads, bending forward in the most uncomfortable

RENNES.

position, and apparently quite absorbed. Their eyes never wandered; not a joint in their body stirred. There were many women, domestic servants, girls from the country, and one or two nuns. Their figures and faces were like those of mediæval saints in the cathedral niches. I saw no excitement or eagerness; they were simply overmastered. It was the absolute intensity of their belief, as though they had been taken to see the Emperor at the Tuileries, all in the glitter of gold, and a chamberlain had bid them kneel and be quiet. Is this sort of religion anything else than a constraining fear? Have these good folk any idea of absolute justice?

Near Thabor there is a large chapel, with the Virgin and infant Jesus on the altar, both crowned. She is indeed both queen and goddess. It looks, at times, as though Catholicism were a revival of polytheism, with unhappy and tender persons worshipped in place of strong ones.

Gradually the type of the race impresses one. There is a feature especially conspicuous in the peasant women, children, and young girls in the market. It is not a regular beauty, either of health or of fine development, but a certain acuteness of form, a look of endurance, pallor, suppression. In many young girls, however, this creates an expression which compels admiration. It marks a perfect form of virginity, of the senses and of the soul, an exquisite sensibility, a charming delicacy, prone to suffering through its very excess, and a remarkable gentleness. It reminds one of the Indian saying, "Do not strike a woman, even with a flower." It is an inner beauty; the soul is reluctant, resigned, frail, infinitely soft.

During a ride in the park, on the day of my arrival, I saw an engaged couple walking out with the parents of the devoted swain. The girl wore a tall hat with stiff trimmings, white and embroidered, like a survival from a fifteenth-century head-dress. She had a brown skirt, a figure without a waist, reminding one of the thirteenth-century statues, a little violet shawl, in keeping with the rest, and black stockings. Her face was rather small, but the pretty grey eyes were full of candour. It was not the simple candour of a German or an English woman. This was none of your commanding, fresh, high-coloured, buxom girls; on the contrary she was short, and her arms and neck were too thin. Surely to such a type must have belonged the pure heroines of old-world Breton chivalry, the mystic love of the tales that tell of the Holy Grail, of Percival, Elaine, Yolande, and Geraint. Renan has written finely of this delicate and enduring sensibility of the Celtic races.

On the other hand, the soldier who directed me

to the barracks assured me that no country is more easy-going.

"In the daytime they will not look at you, but at night they are affable enough."

And that is what it comes to in the Breton romances, and in the British lands generally, in the Middle Age. We read of a priest with ten wives, and others had still more.

There were six tipsy men asleep on the church steps. They had drunk four litres of cider, with brandy to follow. In all the outlying quarters of the town there was dirt, bad smells, and penury. Not till six years ago did they begin to erect decent houses. Several districts reminded me of the Ghetto at Frankfort. Everything is dirty here, even the hotel, though it is the best in the town, and very expensive. It has a yard in common with another hotel, which receives and despatches parcels; there is no end to the bustle, the beggars, and so forth. My own hotel is an old-fashioned city tavern, with lofty rooms, old furniture picked up at sales, the paper peeling from the walls, and bad smells everywhere. What a contrast to Douai!

The Lycée had seven hundred pupils. The bishop established a religious college, and on one day half of the students left. Now the Lycée is in a languishing state.

THE MUSEUM AT RENNES.

The pictures come partly from a private collection of the Marquis de ——. They are the property of the nation, brought here at the time of the Revolution. The rest are an overflow from the Paris museums. In 1804 the Louvre was more than full, and some of the canvases were sent to the provincial museums.

The building in which they are housed is the old Lecture Theatre. There is a museum of conchology, of casts, of miscellaneous pictures, and terra cottas of different periods, scattered here and there. One canvas was given by the Emperor, "La pauvre femme déposant son enfant au tour," which was bought at the Exposition of 1858. Everything is clean and new as an artificial tooth. The idea occurred to me again and again; the barracks, the court-house, the university, all without roots of their own, all planted in. For instance, there are no painters at Rennes—only drawing-masters and a few amateurs. The notion returns when you come upon a grand building, recently sprung up, conspicuous, or out of harmony with its surroundings. Thanks to some ministerial arrangement, funds have been voted in Paris; a Parisian architect has been sent down; he has done his business, and the town is richer by a block.

Nevertheless, there is some good in the system. All the imbeciles, peasants, and poor townsfolk have officials assigned to them, just as the Hindoos receive their Anglo-Indian civil servants. If it were not for that, there would be no good roads, no administration of justice, and no schools.

After my examinations I went into the Museum, and that cleared my mind. It is not a bad thing to have an occupation in order to understand what occupation means, and thereby to understand what the majority of men have in their heads. Only you must not be too long over your occupation.

There are two Wynants and a few other Dutch pictures. I like them better every year; they have painted a normal condition of things, and even an ideal condition—quiet, comfort, and contentment. Nowadays, painters recognise the violent, strange, or poetic side of nature, but their peasants are no more than physiological studies. The future in every art is for such as select or meet with subjects which all succeeding generations will approve. Happiness is one of these themes, but nervous disorder and psychological peculiarities are not amongst them. I could not perceive the beauty of happiness until I was well advanced in life. In the early days this did not come home to me, or I thought it stale.

Wynants has a delicate soul, somewhat melancholy, but still charming. His tints are soft, or rather softened. He has two gracefully drooping birch-trees, many trees growing slightly out of shape, still and lustrous water, light foliage taking on the hues of evening, fleecy clouds floating gradually upwards, piling grey on satin folds, tawny stretches of soil, pale distances melting hue in hue, a damp coolness spreading through the air, a languid peace stealing over and enfolding everything with a caress.

In judging a landscape, the whole question is one of more or less moisture in the air. My temperament needs more than a Roman or a Greek would demand. After a brief time, face to face with a southern literature or art, my sensibility is wounded, and I require an imperceptible humidity in the atmosphere to allay the scorching heat of their sun.

A *Horse-fair* of Wouvermans. The spacious reach of sky and air is filled with a fine mist, pervaded by sunshine; the splendid horses, covered with brown or white horsecloths, throw up their heads, or display their glossy, well-nourished limbs. All the buyers are dressed in velvet or bright yellow silk, with satin ribbons, bands and rosettes, and large top-boots.

They are magnificently handsome in their wide-brimmed hats, swords, wigs and lace sleeves, though a trifle heavy in appearance. The ladies are stiff-looking in their white satin skirts. But it is still unmistakably a last scene in the knightly, aristocratic life described in the "Memoirs" of Bostaquet. What a parade it was! How happy they were in that emancipation from ideas and refinement! It is easy to be seen, in Dumont de Bostaquet, that feasting and parade, hunting and pomp and circumstance, sufficed for happiness.

A *Vierge au chardonneret*, by Van Herp, one of the pupils of Rubens. This is a charming girl, somewhat affected in style, with long tapering fingers; but it is an essentially good picture. There is such an effusion of love in the soft, deep tones of the hair and shoulders. The child, round and pink as a flower, has lips like cherries, and no thought but for the breast. He has the serious look peculiar to children; he is but recently born, and has very little hair. There is a drop of milk awaiting him, and his lips are exactly shaped for the teat.

Clearly the underlying principle of this school of painting is not the same as with us. They painted to please some rich and tranquil burgher, living in comfort and adorning his house. We paint for the cross at the Exposition, or to make a name, to be talked about, to stimulate the jaded taste of a few Parisians or cosmopolitans, critics and their readers, and men about town.

A *Moonlight* by Van der Neer. This is a marvellous effect. It is another of his great low-banked rivers; in the foreground an old willow, showing the ravages of time, and two fishermen; in the shadow a number of half-concealed boats, and the omnipresent humidity, that rises between the earth and the sky. The marvellous effect is the superabundance of the fog. It is exhaled from stream and land alike; the mists swell out and expand themselves in fold on fold, floating slowly on the ubiquitous vapour, above the parent water, which engenders them continually and for ever. The vast and murky night which shrouds the whole earth collects and mingles its flocks; every varying shape swims up and disappears in its glooming depths, now black, now indigo, like the swollen water of a sluggish canal.

Mark the difference in the contemporary landscapes in the other room, Chaigneau, Anastasi, Pinguilly, Blin, etc. The old school of painting seized on fundamental realities, and made the most of them; the modern painter seizes on the conspicuous accident, the differentiating mark, and aims at reproducing the effect. Thus the *Dutch Landscape* of Anastasi is thoroughly true in its unpleasant bluish-green grass and its strange dissolving sky of bluish-black. That strikes us by contrast with our French sky. But Anastasi did not love Holland, and he missed the essential, the lasting, the welcome features which are the discoveries of love.

There are two examples of Crayer. The *Resurrection of Lazarus* is signed and dated 1664. It has an almost Venetian delicacy of soft and melting hues, glimmerings of pink light, flesh tints passing into each other, or into the shadow, glints of sunshine in hair of red gold, or in gauzy falls of lace. Note the sister of Lazarus, with her beautiful shapely hands, her full throat, smooth as satin, surmounted by a richly moulded chin and deep flushed cheeks, and her dark blue skirt of satin, lustrous beneath a hood of golden damask. What a kindly and gracious lady! No painters can surpass the Flemings, except the Venetians themselves. This picture is much better blended, and more voluptuous in colour, than the *Christ on the Cross;* and it seems to be the work of a Flemish admirer of the Venetian school. It is at once real and idealised. Crayer has not a great reputation, because he has been in some sense left out of account: Rubens has smothered him. And in this *Christ on the Cross* he is indeed far from the modern studies of anguish and of psychological refinement.

Jordaens also has a *Christ on the Cross*, admirably finished and expressive. There is no movement. The Christ is open-eyed, and tastes in silence the bitterness of death. There are fine and luminous flesh-tones on a dark background. The extreme beauty of the picture is due to this magnificence of the bright flesh-tones thrown out upon a dark sky, and to the profoundly true expression, and to the human types copied from the life. I have seen examples of this great painter at Mayence, la Haye, and Antwerp. We do not know him at Paris, where we possess nothing but one of his drolleries.

There is one Dutch picture, however, which is absolutely sublime—*The Newborn Child*, attributed to Lenain. Two women are gazing at a week-old baby, fast asleep. All that physiology has to say about the first phase of humanity is there! Words cannot express the child's profound, absorbing sleep, like the sleep it slept a week ago, without hair or eyelashes, its lower lip drawn down, its nostrils and mouth open, mere gateways of the breath, its bright skin without a fold, scarce touched as yet by the air, still as it were a simple graft of vegetative life.

The upper lip is curled back; it has no function but to breathe. The tiny body is clasped and bound in its stiff white swaddling-clothes like a mummy in its shroud. There could be no better expression to indicate this primitive torpor, this soul not yet summoned from its tomb. All this is thrown into relief by the dull presence of the mother, by the simple crudity of the strong red dress which casts its warm reflection on the little mass of plump flesh.

The impression of inertness, of a mere mass of breathing flesh, is increased as we note the round unshaped nose, red with its pulsing veins, and the skin, so delicate that you might suppose it to be non-existent. The forehead is absolutely smooth, without a fold or a wrinkle, fat, shining, rounded, all sheathed in flesh; the whole face equally smooth with its vegetation of flesh—flesh so soft that the slightest finger-touch would make a little pit. Nothing but the vigour of the vitality of birth could expand and hold together a pulp so elastic and so humid. The closing of the eyelids is indicated by the scarcely perceptible chink which divides them; the light lashes are imperceptible, even if their growth has begun. The pink of the face deepening into purple, lymphatic and sanguine, wax-like and almost fluent, is in contrast with its crude white, and with the long linen wrap which completely enfolds him. And the whole effect is heightened by the thoroughly Flemish aspect of the young mother, with her quiet sheepish features, and by the heifer-like stolidity of the middle-aged woman who holds the light.

The dominant impression here is that this genuine painter is a simple body-artist. The subject is insignificant; but with what closeness and profundity he has grasped the physical reality, with all its life and colouring! The more genuine an artist is, the more constantly and assiduously he labours to reproduce the actual.

The *Woman taken in Adultery*, by Loth, is an admirable piece of Flemish realism. The rich sensuous woman, in her bodice of dark flesh-colour and her yellow drapery, the soft bosom, the painted eyes and pouting expression, stupid-looking amidst the vulgar and hilarious mockers who surround her, is quite a study of the lymphatic and sanguine Flemish temperament. In eyes such as those, tears have not the same effect as in those of our own countrymen. This is still more evident in Jordaens' *Christ on the Cross*, which hangs beneath the other.

Dry and cold is the *Magdalen*, of Philippe de Champagne, a psychologist's well-bred lady. A painter is nothing if not an expert in temperament.

The *Andromeda and Perseus* of Veronese. Andromeda stands undraped, with one knee bent, restless, enveloped in gray shadows; her foot and knee are flushed with light; her red robe has slipped from its knot, and fallen beside her. It is a picture of the voluptuous, refined rather than commonplace voluptuousness. Well might they dally away two or three centuries, with their music, and women like that! Nowhere could you find a more exquisite ear, or lovelier locks under such strings of pearls, or flesh of such perfect contour, so sensitive to the touch. Perseus, with averted face, floats towards her through the clear sky; beneath, a grey city shows across the waves, with bridges and turrets like those of Venice. It is an admirable background; bold and strange is the motion of the warrior, glittering in his garment of lustrous violet and yellow.

This type is supplemented by a *Massacre of the Innocents*, with its vehement confusion and multiplicity of attitudes. It is fertile in suggestion and full of animation, though in a different sense from that of Raphael's work. We are in another world, where beauty is full of marrow, not deformed and overcast with the ugliness of realism, as in Flanders, but ample and charmingly rounded. Here are full well-turned throats, and shoulders substantial though tender, which claim our admiration; hair drawn slightly away from the face, delicately shortened noses, dainty ears, eyes full of challenge, all showing the character and quality of these beautiful forms.

A *Louis Treize Ballet* is the work of Abraham Bosse, of the seventeenth century. In the costumes there is a reminiscence of the display of Matamore, and the rough trooper of the civil wars. The same roughness is still more conspicuous in the *Ball at the Court of the Valois*. The cavaliers clasp the ladies firmly, so as to be ready for a jump, in the style of a village dance. Those who are seated hold them on their knees, with their arms round their waists. All the men are lively, brainless fellows. One, with his back to us, shows his profile, with reddish beard and moustache. Another, dressed in white silk, and wearing an enormous ruff, with pearls in his ears, a genuine type of the period of Henry III., is a sort of well-bred assassin, gay and cruel as Coconas. They are nimble as greyhounds, and their costume heightens the effect; it clings to the body and sets off the figure, shows up the muscles and emphasizes their strength and agility; it is just the thing for jumping, wrestling, or fencing. The thick braided doublet is as good as a breastplate. The cloak bespeaks the hard rider, and so does the plumed and broad-brimmed hat. Some wear high narrow-brimmed hats, adorned by tufts sprinkled with gold. This dress of bright contrasted colours supports at once the idea of brutal jollity and habitual display; the women, buried in their enormous dresses and cylindrical sleeves, have the same empty-headed appearance. When they want to dance they have to leap vigorously; and they are correspondingly unwieldy in the hands of their partners. In brief, they are contemporaries of Brantôme, a sorry rout of vigorous, base, and sensual creatures.

Mytens (1636-1688) affords a marked and instructive contrast in his *Feast in honour of Marie de Gonzague*, when she was departing for the home of her husband, the King of Poland. Its delicacy and simplicity are charming, and reveal the first phase of a new ceremonial dignity and decency, as well as the Dutch quietude of existence. The costumes are plain and honest. The age of Louis Quatorze is at hand.

In the Library of Rennes I made acquaintance with sundry Lives of the Saints, popular stories and poems, collected by Hersent de la Villemarqué, and a volume of "Mœurs de Bretagne," a collection of 1794, continued by Souvestre.

Here is an episode from the life of a Breton saint, which aptly illustrates the savagery of the feudal age, the tyranny of a strong and solitary man, with no control apart from his individual whims. A seigneur has seen a beautiful girl, whom he wishes to marry. The father, himself a lord, refuses his consent, on the ground that the other is in the habit of slaying his wives as soon as they are in the way of becoming mothers. The saint obtains from the seigneur a promise that he will treat the maiden well; and then the marriage takes place, and he loves her passionately. She goes the way of her predecessors, and then he begins to grumble, and eyes her askance. She is alarmed, and rides off on horseback, that her child may be born at her father's castle. The husband pursues her in his rage, and, though she conceals herself in a wood, he tracks her like a wolf after a hind, and cuts off her head. The saint arrives on the spot, replaces the head, and bids her rise; which command she obeys. She tells him that she had been in heaven, but resumed her body at his word. Her child is born at her father's castle; after which she becomes a nun for the rest of her days, and her son was St Travers.

The morals of the Bretons are still very primitive.

Whole families go into the towns once a week, visit a tavern, and drink all day until they can drink no more. Then one of them, who has bargained to remain all but sober, lays the rest in his cart, and drives them home.

Souvestre has described a wedding-feast. There are five hundred at table, each with a glass, a plate, and a wooden spoon. They go on eating for three or four hours, as quick as they can, using both hands, gorging themselves red in the face, like wolves at a feast; and then they smoke and dance. That is like the Arabs, when they light on a sheep after long fasting.

FROM RENNES TO LE MANS AND TOURS.

THE country is transformed; the wild and succulent verdure ceases. There are no more oaks; the moisture grows less abundant. We pass the Loir, and presently come in sight of the Loire.

There is a wide plain, a stream with no defined course, which is often in flood and often runs partly dry, amidst cyots of shingle and long banks of sand. The sandbanks have a certain vegetation, and there are broad lands covered with stunted pines.

But, especially after passing Tours, nothing could be more cheerful, or give better indication of comfort and prosperity. There are beautiful meadows, abundant crops, fruit trees, and rows of poplars, with every now and then a peaceful farm. Hemp, corn, various kinds of fruit, are plentiful; there is no more buckwheat, as in Brittany. The sky adds to the pleasantness and cheerfulness of the country. The velvet southern sky begins at this point, a radiant blue infused with light, like the clearest crystal. This lovely colour, sparkling and tender, sheds a glow of happiness over the trees, over the long stretch of fertile fields; the whole landscape resembles a garden, not the formal, plotted, economised garden of England, but somewhat casually tended, with a suggestion of neglect, though man's light-hearted negligence robs him of no whit of earth's prodigality. A few white castles, with picturesque turrets, perched like pigeons amongst the foliage, raise their blue pointed roofs and survey the plain from their vantage-ground. They bring to mind the happy life of the Valois, and Diana of Poitiers, and Francis I. and Rabelais, the careless, gallant ways of life, the hunting, the boating-parties on those bright and wayward streams. This was the very scene for the beauties of Jean Goujon, Germain Pilon, Primatice, Rosso, the fine voluptuous heads, the bound hair, the dainty limbs that would be ever peeping from behind their drapery!

I passed the night at Tours. There is a fine wide street, crowded and full of shops, quite in the style of Paris, with the same tattoo, drums, trumpets, noisy clash of sound, with overwhelming din of popular amusements, in which everyone seemed to be taking a part. An unmistakable contrast to Rennes.

I rose at five in the morning, in order to see the

Cathedral. The porch is very fine and rich, well carved, with two towers ending in blunted points; but there is too much exaggeration of the Gothic. Stone lacework everywhere—mere filigree; you would not get more delicate and manifold mouldings in a drawing-room. The consequence is that nothing fixes the attention. Many of the apertures and windows have been built in to arrest the crumbling of the stone; on the right hand an enormous patch of masonry has been clapped on in wretched fashion from ground to roof. There is the same thing at Strasbourg, where the framework of the belfry is of iron, the stone just concealing it. This is vulgarised and debased art. Mediæval civilisation is all like that, showy and hollow.

Nothing is sound; incongruity is everywhere. The apse is a sort of pigeon-cote, tiled with slates. There are many buttresses encroaching on the street, like dislocated claws of a crab, to bolster up some protuberance or other. The interior is fine, lofty, and full of ideas. The painted windows struck me most. The morning sun glowed in the large windows of the apse like a radiant resurrection dawn; the three roses began to sparkle, more gorgeous than a peacock's tail; but the effect was quite of a different order, full of vehemence and pain. These colours have a voice; they are all in excess, bright yellow, scarlet, a great mass of deep violet, the most tragic of all hues, which ought to be before our eyes in our moments of ecstasy.

I remember a beautiful group at Poitiers, in the right aisle of the cathedral, apparently fifteenth century, almost contemporary with the first of the Solesmes statues. It is an Entombment. The Christ, full-bearded, a wretched earth-worm, emaciated by grief, dried up, wasted in body, a mere skeleton under a skin, shrunken and discoloured by wounds, caked with blood: such was the Man of Sorrows whom the fillers of these rose-lights had in their minds.

The day before yesterday I saw the foundry of Ruelle. I noted a few interesting facts. The workmen earn from twenty-six to fifty sous a day; half of them have accumulated some property, from fifteen to fifty thousand francs, perhaps a little carriage, but generally a house. An American Colonel who was visiting the place said to me:

"That is the best of France: they are better off than their fellows in any other country. Above all, they do not dream of leaving the ranks."

It is the southern aristocratic type all over; and he is right. These people have acquired their ideal since the Revolution—a patch of land. Their ambition does not rise beyond it; an occasional good dinner, and no very heavy taxes. France is made for them.

On the other hand, ambitions are much limited. There are two young men of five-and-twenty, one a rich farmer's son, the other the son of a well-to-do proprietor, who are designers at the foundry on forty sous a day.

The townspeople, again, are shut off from the world; their life has no amplitude, no connecting links. You might compare them to so many little jars of stagnant water; no one is in full evidence. The Colonel says that our manners here are peculiar to ourselves. Frenchmen's doors are closed to foreigners, except for a few compulsory receptions of persons high in office. What a contrast to English and American hospitality! In the United States you bring a letter of introduction to a single person, and before the day is over you receive a score of visiting cards; the American has been exhorting his friends to see you, and already twenty hospitable houses are open to you.

"All we know of France is Paris," says the Colonel; and that is true. Even at Paris we draw the line at verbal politeness. There is half-an-hour's pleasant conversation, and that is all. Receptions are impossible; life is too full of occupation, our houses are two small, and our manner of living too restricted. At the utmost we take our guest to a restaurant; we mistrust ourselves, and lock up our minds. Hospitality is an aristocratic virtue.

I find myself coming back again and again to this idea, that France is a democracy of peasants and working-men under a motherly administration, with a restricted town population which lives cheaply and grows rusty, and with needy officials who are on the look-out for promotion, and never take root.

BORDEAUX.

THE change of type is remarkable. It had already begun to change at Ruelle. It may be looked for especially in the young women. Here there is something which is both delicate and sprightly. In a child, still fresh to life and modest, the effect is charming. The white cap adds to the gathered knot of hair, which stands high and prominent behind, somewhat in the style of 1830. This attractive white crest, trim and clean, throws out the delicate, intelligent face, slightly browned, and without much colour. The neck is slender, the eyes black, the body slim; and one cannot but be pleased with the intelligent brightness of the type.

These features are yet more strongly marked at Bordeaux. Accent, looks, figure, all change together. The people are short and full of movement; their bearing and their gait remind you of rats, of nimbly scurrying mice. The poorest girls wear their clothes coquettishly, with many a flaunt and turn to show

THEATRE AT BORDEAUX.

off their figure. The kerchief on their heads is elegantly arranged.

This town is a sort of second Paris, gay and magnificent, with wide streets, promenades, monuments, and large mansions. The streets are bustling and full of carriages; there is no lack of coaches, of fine toilettes, or of money. Amusement is the main business, in marked contrast to Rennes. C——, who has lived here four years, after spending eleven months at Rennes, said that when he first came he thought himself in Paradise. In short, the life is gay, much in evidence, wholly of a southern cast; whilst the trade of the place, largely concerned with wine, keeps plenty of money circulating.

They are right to amuse themselves. Since I have been following an occupation I know what an occupation means. One wants to turn one's back on it, to forget the dulness and monotony of business, to give all the senses their draught of champagne. The life of the artist or the author is of quite another kind. He has had his joy, has created, has done a man's work all day, and wants to rest in the evening.

I was over-tired. I had seen nothing, even on my ride from Tours, except vague and misty forms, evening after evening, infinitely sad and touching, and except, also, the smiling district of Ruelle—the vines on every hill, the glittering meadows in the low-lying lands; fresh water in the lavish streams, with reeds and luxuriant water plants; poplars on every hand, with a strange emerald glow in the shade beneath them, pierced by the flashing and breaking darts of the sun; here and there bright lights in the background. At a distance, low sloping roofs with light-coloured tiles, an occasional windmill, a venerable church with its picturesque village, such as one sees in Italy, on the edge of a clear blue lake.

I have been several times at Bourdeax; I have seen and described the river and the excellent port.[1] To-day, between two showers of rain, I walked in the Botanic Garden, which is new to me. There is a placid, green-banked river, plantations of young bananas, fine well-arranged trees, as in the London parks. But the neighbouring houses are too conspicuous.

The main thing to look at here is the people. The students whom I saw have a ready and decided manner; they invent when they do not know. They are glib-tongued, original, and ingenious. Their heads are well shaped, often sharp featured, and always active. How different from the sleepy candidates at La Flèche!

The accent is remarkable. One feels inclined to

---

[1] *Voyage aux Pyrénées.*

ask them: "Have you had your breakfast, Jacquot?" Their pronunciation is crisp and rolling; they show great volubility, and there is a sing-song from time to time in their utterance.

The people exhibit an independent familiarity. I wore a black hat and gloves, and carried a brief-case under my arm. I asked my way of an old oyster-woman. "There you are, my friend, close by!" she said, and gave me a pat on the shoulder. It must be added that she took a few steps and put herself to some trouble in order to show me the street. That has happened to me several times here. At the hotel, the waiters speak to us, and even to our Colonel himself, with an air of equality, making remarks on the qualities of the dishes which they bring us.

There was an amusing scene as I was on my way to Cenon. I was looking for the omnibus, and came upon a crowd of fiacres, coaches, and other vehicles. A good ten drivers descended upon me. "Where are you going? Here you are! . . . Cinquanté sous, quarranté sous, trennté sous. . . . I'll take you to the foot of the hill. . . . I'm going quite close; I know the house; it's the only house I do know. . . . Get in! . . . Am I to take you? . . . Ténez, violà une placé, uné bonné placé." It was a regular inundation. I take an omnibus, and repeat my question. Thereupon an endless flood of assurances. In the end he lands me, saying that the place was within two minutes. A washerwoman hard by declares that it is twenty minutes off. This puts him into a storm of indignation; he springs from his seat, turns as red as a cock, gesticulates, harangues the washerwoman, appeals to the other people in the omnibus. I had walked on some fifty steps, but still I heard his shrill voice and saw his swinging arms. He had lied to me, with the imagination and ready invention of the southern race. On the road, he had jumped down at every turning to adjust a trace, or to talk to his horse. He had a cigar in his mouth; he was ragged and dirty; the wretched vehicle was drawn by ropes, attached to a sorry yellow hack.

They take no trouble about anything here; they let everything slide, and make shift as they go along. The basis of their character is the necessity and the habit of immediate expansion; as soon as an idea occurs to them, it finds vent with an exaggeration which is not a little ridiculous. It is the temper of the marionette. With this they are satisfied, asking for nothing more than easy, instantaneous excitement and reproduction—to go out, to dance, to frequent the café, to walk about, to talk, and laugh, and gesticulate. The French character is much more marked and even exaggerated here than elsewhere.

In Paris there is quite another spirit. I meet two caricatures in the street, and instantly feel myself two hundred leagues away. A husband (with an enormous nose) holds his six months' baby in his arms, whilst his wife, a woman of thirty, combs her hair and tidies herself. With a comic look of desolation he exclaims: "Jove, if I were to take myself seriously!" (Si l'on réfléchissait, crénom!) The companion picture is that of the husband duped. The Parisian spirit is not merely external, it goes to the root of things, and has its element of immoral philosophy. Look at Daumier, Marcelin, Gavarni, Marlotte's men and women. There are ideas behind their cheerfulness; and the cheerfulness itself is often only apparent or transient. The real basis is that of sceptical ideas.

I had a fine view of Cenar, thanks to the grandeur, or rather the breadth of the landscape; but there was nothing characteristic. It was but a chart of physical geography. The golden splendour, the red conflagration of the setting sun amongst the streaks of luminous mist, were its only beauty.

FROM BORDEAUX TO TOULOUSE.

THIS is a flat country, all under cultivation. I saw but a single wood in a railway ride of six hours. There were no hills, or other prominent features, not even a wide plain. All was petty and commonplace. You could say, "'Tis a fine country," and have done with it.

Certain alluvial soils, formed by the Garonne, are worth fifteen thousand francs the hectare; they grow corn, tobacco, and hemp. Those I saw are of an average type, and yield about two and a half per cent. on the capital.

There are frequent glimpses of the Garonne on the right, yellow or reddish-brown from the sands. The banks are lined by pale osier-beds. Then, between its two raised banks, we get sight of the Southern Canal, the aspect of which is not charming, however great its utility. There is wide variety of industry, small fields, belonging to different proprietors, and, I am told, not very grand results.

The division of the land has destroyed the landscape.

The houses here are interesting, thanks to the neighbourhood of Italy and the balmy climate. The roofs are almost flat; and there is no snow in winter. Many houses have two wings, which gives them a character of their own. Some are surrounded by columns, and have long balconies, built out if necessary to secure a western aspect. The belfries are square, a few of the newer ones standing out with much effect; and, under this clear sky and brilliant light, their clean white tapering forms are very attractive. The bells are not enclosed within four walls, but a single wall is built, with apertures, and on this they are hung. Now and then there is a tower; and there are a few châteaux, with turrets and flagstaffs. In all this there is a measure of architectural taste.

Yet I cannot help feeling, for my own part, that my best and truest pleasure will always come from the forests and streams. I am a man of the North, not of the South.

TOULOUSE.

YESTERDAY, in the public square, I took stock of sundry folk. There are seats under the arcades, the cafés are full, the square is occupied by kiosques and laurel trees; there is abundance of life and movement.

I passed five or six times in front of a couple of girls. One was decidedly pretty. She was a working girl, of fine figure, dressed in a yellow print, with a handsome bust, and back hair drawn away from her head. They were talking well and without restraint, with a natural grace. The old shopkeeper next to them was having a good time of it. You would almost take them, at first, for ladies. The Southerner possesses a sort of education by virtue of his origin; he is saved from coarseness by his birth. The face is regular, of a light-brown complexion. You are predisposed to find a real beauty, more than skin-deep, and you anticipate a keen spirit, genuine wit, not to say nobility of character. After a quarter of an hour the substratum shows itself; all is superficial in this type of beauty and spirit. They are graceful, with the vivacity of a bird—of a delicate twittering tomtit; but there is nothing more in their cackle. If you wish to please them you must take them to a ball, feed them, crack jokes, talk a great deal, and make them talk still more; go with them to listen to the dance music and military bands. "Ah! how much more beautiful are the stars when they mirror themselves in the gutter of the Rue du Bac!" They make me think of poor Heine's Juliette, when he had his odd experience with her in the Pyrenees.

The Parisian girl is of another type—more adaptable, more disposed to hover on the outskirts of luxury and corruption.

STROLLS IN TOULOUSE.

I AM without sympathy for the people of this town. There is a yelp, a shrill metallic ring, in the accent. You feel, as you see them move about and accost each other, as though you were amongst a different race—a mixture of pug-dog and ape, a hollow facility, an unconscious and perpetual exaggeration, a never-ceasing want of tact. For instance: a lawyer and a boarding-house master came pestering us with a demand to enter the examination-room at their pleasure.

My impression on the parade yesterday was that these good folk need to be governed from without. They are utterly incapable of self-control. Blood, excitement, anger, rise to their heads on the slightest pretext. I was told how near they came, in 1841, to making an end of M. Plougoulm, the procureur-général.

The further I go, the more I am convinced of the downward tendency of our democracy. Its atmosphere is fatal to men of high standing and wide culture; we have monstrosities and powerful machines, nothing more; we rest on a mere foundation of respectabilities; we have reached an ideal, but it is a poor ideal. In fine, the man of high standing is the man of leisure, who has no trade, who is only half devoted to his private interest, who is concerned with broad views, who takes the lead, like the English aristocracy of our own days, or the Roman and Greek of other times. If this aristocracy is to endure and conciliate, it must devote its strength and its time to the public service. Also, it must seek out the best products of the other classes. A legislator should recognise that it is his duty to bring to the front the finest and most perfect samples of humanity, to select them as from a herd, to cultivate a higher grade of boys and girls, both morally and physically superior in heart and brain, endowed with knowledge, free to develop their faculties, exempt from the mechanical drudgery of mere bread-winning. That done, the remainder of the herd must browse quietly and securely, led and cared for by the others. We must give an excellent start, honour, easy circumstances, the chance of founding a family, all the higher objects of human ambition, to proved merit, wherever it may be found. The start amongst ourselves is inadequate ; but there is a moderate start for moderate merit.

It may be urged, on the other hand, that a country is like a garden, that one product may be finer and better than another, but that all gardens cannot grow it; that all depends on sun and aspect, so that a good gardener knows what he is about beforehand; that it is absurd to seek pine-apples from the chalk of Champagne, and that France, in short, is now growing the plants which it is able to produce. For high-bred souls the remedy is to avoid sinking into the commonplace form of existence, and to live apart, like Woepke in his Buddhism.[1]

The quays are fine; water is always fine. There is a great mill of several storeys, and several watercourses, set in a framework of trees and shrubs. A large lock unites the streams again in the middle of the river. The red buildings glow in the setting sun, with bright or softened hues. Opposite is an old hospital with strange narrow windows, but great and imposing; its high discoloured wall, with its poor array of lights, overhangs the river boldly, in mediæval fashion.

Behind it is the great dome of St Nicholas, which at nightfall assumed a sinister appearance.

Higher up the stream is a long, solid bridge of stone, flanked at the approach by two square towers, running to a point at the top in the style of Louis XIII. Originally, no doubt, they were for purposes of defence.

The hills rise towards the south. The sky is so clear that in the far distance the chain of the Pyrenees looks like a white bed of watery clouds. The river, dressed in smiling verdure, skirts along

---

[1] See the account of Franz Woepke, in the *Nouveaux Essais de Critique et d Histoire*, p. 317.

them. It has reminded me of my beautiful journey —beautiful though sad; and all that was ideal about it I have set down in my book.[1] So it is always; there are only a few landscapes which, at some moments, look supremely beautiful. As a rule, our sensations are rudimentary, mere *motifs* of a cavatina. If they are to be perfect, we must correct and complete them. I feel it now again. Here and there a façade, a few old houses of wood and clay, a few Renaissance turrets and Gothic churches — but it would be necessary to elaborate the picture.

Yesterday, however, the church of St Étienne, at six o'clock in the evening, struck me as full of grandeur and melancholy. It is all irregular, and collapsing on one side. But in the dim interior there was a vast collection of large paintings and carvings, begrimed and indistinct in contrast with the fitful gleams of light. I cannot find words to describe these unfathomable, vague, tremulous, Rembrandt-like obscurities, this imposing shipload of ghosts. The rose-window still retained a half-gleam of light, saddening and mystical with its violet-hued carnations, its strange confused forms, the last scintillations of its dolorous magnificence.

---

[1] *Voyage aux Pyrénées.*

It was like a dream of heaven that visits by night a loving and tormented soul.

I walked frequently through the town, especially in the evening. It is all awry and misshapen. "It is Poitiers in Sunday best," said the Colonel. But there is movement in the streets, a crowd in the square and at the café; and all wavering in a deep shadow, streaked with light. It is not a dead city, but a provincial centre and capital, proud of itself. There are two widely circulated papers, taken in by the humblest barber and pork-butcher. Here in our hotel, the best in Toulouse, there is not a single Parisian paper. The *Aigle* and the *Journal de Toulouse* are full of local news. Some vocalist known in the neighbourhood is about to make a first appearance at Lyon. Léotard, the gymnast, is here, and they make a boast of that. They have a correspondent, a local gentleman, who discourses on important political questions. I see there are sundry booksellers—one well stocked with new books—refutations of Renan, refutations even of the refutations.

These people pay much attention to their dress. The men are smart and dandified in their appearance, with well-trimmed tufts of beards, and close-buttoned overcoats. They are so many little Italian hairdressers. My soldier yesterday, a man from Bar le Duc, did not spare them.

"They are all liars and scandal-mongers," he said, "and they have no manners."

"How do you mean?"

"Why, at the theatre they hiss all the time, and keep up a devil's tattoo. They are mere brutes. But they have a respect for soldiers, or there would be any amount of trouble."

In the streets you see the most unconsciously ridiculous figures and attitudes amongst the braggarts and bullies of the place. Still more frequently you are struck by their delightful self-complacency like that of Molière's Acaste:—

> J'ai du bien, je suis jeune, et sors d'une maison
> Qui se peut dire noble avec quelque raison . . .
> Et l'on m'a vu pousser, dans le monde, une affaire
> D'une assez vigoureuse et gaillarde manière . . .
> Je suis assez adroit, j'ai bon air, bonne mine,
> Les dens belles surtout, et la taille fort fine.
> Quant à se mettre bien, je crois, sans me flatter,
> Qu'on serait mal venu de me le disputer.

The "gentleman" is a rarity in France. A host of important persons, officials and landowners, come crawling to us on behalf of their sons, begging us to rob somebody else of his position to give it to them.¹ Whether they do it with a brazen face or with circumlocution, it is still a demand that we should act unjustly. They consider that such partiality would be perfectly natural; and they have the same idea of unfairness in examinations. Copying went on at this centre in the most unblushing fashion. My colleagues told me that the South has always been less scrupulous in examinations than the North. It is traditional in France; under the old Monarchy it was quite the thing to beg favours of the judges. To this day you do not gain admission to the public Journals if you have no friends upon them. In England, on the contrary, my friend C—— told me that you could never thank an editor for inserting your article: it would annoy him. Carlyle, in his life of John Sterling, quotes a letter of Sir Robert Peel's to the editor of the *Times*, and the reply that was sent. This is the land of favours, but the other is a land of justice.

I have seen many old houses out of repair, tiled roofs, a strange medley of ill-assorted houses in

---

¹ There is plenty of comedy about these examinations. One father brings his son before the time, in order that he may get to know the Colonel's face. Another leaves flasks of oil with the porter, as presents for the examiners. We had to transfer them to the police commissioner.

every style of building. The paving is of wretched little pointed stones, river shingle, which is painful to walk upon. But the charm and serenity of the sky the pure and brillant azure, are admirable.

I took a walk yesterday under the guidance of M. B——, Professor of History at the University. He is fifty-five, and looks forty. He is a Liberal, and moves in good aristocratic society, is well off, has artistic tastes, and is a devoted antiquarian. As we walked he had much to say about the general condition of things. At Toulouse there are seventy-seven religious houses in a population of a hundred thousand, including three great colleges, one of them containing five hundred students. When Frère Léotard was convicted, many people regarded him as a martyr; in the following year there was an increase of thirty or forty students. At Poitiers there are thirty-eight religious houses in a population of thirty-five thousand. There and at Rennes the lycées have lost half their pupils through competition. I myself saw at Bordeaux, six years ago, a big handsome building which was being constructed for a clerical college. One such building here cost two million francs. At Paris the religious schools enter seventy or eighty pupils at Saint-Cyr every year, and they form a separate clique. Even at paltry towns like Rethel they monopolise everything, and starve the little municipal colleges. All this change has come about since 1852, mainly through the Jesuits. M. Billault spoke in the Chamber of the bequests of which the Government has cognizance, amounting to millions every year. And how much is there which is never declared?

We do not consider all this at Paris. We live in a little world of cultured and intellectual sceptics, and lose sight of the vast public, the vast France. We authors ought to know these things better than anybody. What can the black-coated, well-gloved, provincial tradesman, official, nobleman, country gentleman, or landowner, be expected to read? Next to nothing. They are outside our sphere. The clerical net is spread in these stagnant marshes. It is the old ladies, the fathers who have turned Conservative in their dotage, who make these bequests to the clergy. They have no excitement, no mental stimulus; religion, with its pomps and associations, the weight of tradition, the never-ending solemn litany, draw them back into the old routine. This explains the great commotion over the "Life of Jesus"; it was like a stone dropped into a frog-pond.

At table we discussed the probable outcome of this state of things. Will Catholicism dwindle down, as M. Guizot believes, like paganism under Julian, transformed, re-interpreted, assuming a symbolic shape? For my part, I do not believe that a professor in a religious seminary will ever become a critic like Michel Nicolas, or a symbolist like Iamblichus. The most reasonable anticipation is that of a series of plethoras and blood-lettings. Churchmen will enrich themselves during fifty years of peace, and when the revolutions come to a head their property will be confiscated. But these violent periodical purges are not wholesome.

Here the various ranks of society hold themselves apart. There is only one house where they mingle, that of an old lady whom Professor B—— insisted last night on taking me to see. There were many of the poorer nobility, families living on from ten to thirty thousand pounds a year. They spend three months at Toulouse amidst a certain sort of luxury, and economise in the country during the other nine. They make much of the eldest son, and the younger ones do their best to marry money. Their business in life is to fish for heiresses. They follow no calling; the only occupation which they will condescend to think about is that of an officer in the army, and the cavalry for choice. Next to them come the public officials, then the townsfolk, and men who have made a fortune. These men have no culture, and far less politeness than similar persons in the North. They do not spend much on hospitality, but they have their country house and their carriage.

Their morals are bad; you hear of every kind and degree of dissipation. The young moneyed men find nothing else to do. Unhappily the same thing is said about every large provincial town.

The German townsfolk described by Goethe afford a great contrast. I was reading to-night his *Aus meinem Leben*. What harmless manners and cool temperament you may note in the liberties permitted in his days! Young people embrace, exchange tokens of affection, play at marriage, walk out together and address each other familiarly. They must have had nerves of ice!

Professor B—— showed us over the museum. I spoke of it towards the end of my *Voyage aux Pyrénées*. It is charming. It was once a convent. There are two courts surrounded by arcades, which provide a square promenade, separated from the courts by triplet pillars. The courts are full of beautiful green shrubs, and the cloisters are roofed with red tiles; behind them is a lofty brick tower, adorned with little arched windows and small columns. This solid red mass against the splendid blue of the sky gladdens the heart.

It may be observed that the Northern Gothic

never really established itself here. Run through the Italian churches; there is nothing sad, or gloomily fantastic. Even what there is of Gothic in them is transformed, made peaceful, converted into true and almost sober beauty.

The most curious thing in the town is Saint Sernin, a Roman church of the eleventh century. Professor B—— calls it the finest in France. He is a man of the world, but enthusiasm, the unconscious and not unpleasing pride of the antiquarian, display themselves in spite of his habitual modesty. This church is, indeed, vast and curious, and unmixed in style. It is in course of being restored. It is pure Roman, indeed thoroughly Latin, and for this reason it is decidedly interesting. We are here on the border-line of two artistic styles. The Latin element is seen in the full semicircular arcades, with nothing of the ogive; the main dome has the same semicircular arches; the square pillars are destitue of ornament, except that a column in half-relief stands out from the front face of each, defining and supporting the upper dome. This produces an impression of great solidity, simple, sound, and placid, soothing the mind by its regularity and quiet force.

The passage from one style to another is manifest in the altered form of the capitals. Some retain the Greek acanthus, but most of them show a change of

F

foliation, or a barbarian network of tracery and little animals confused together.

There are five domes and aisles, the domes successively diminishing in height from one side of the building to the other. The windows are not very wide, but the walls are very thick; and there is no painted glass. The abundance of rounded curves and massive structures makes a fine appearance, and the transformation of the antique by the elevation of the building, by the gallery, and the cruciform plan of the church, gives a very pleasing effect, and a sensation of novelty and originality.

The upright figures in low relief, encrusted, as it were, around the crypt, are thoroughly primitive, and worthy of the tenth century. They have an Egyptian air, with their stiff limbs, narrow chests, and heads turned awkwardly sideways, almost grotesque in expression. In the apse are statues in barbarian costume, which have more life, and carry one forward to the fifteenth century.

Outside, there is a delightful belfry of five octagonal stages resting on arches, the three lower arcades being rounded, and the upper two pointed. This is novel and fine. Behind is an apse of rounded vaults, rising in tiers, like those at Ravenna and Verona. In short, this is a fine structure, in direct descent from the Roman style, built on a very simple and well-developed idea, like all antique and classical work. The aisles, the successive staging, the belfry, the secondary apses, show the blossoming of the ancient architectural idea. For this idea was developed at the same time with those of society and worship. More space was needed for that new crowd of humanity, with their wives, children, and slaves—a whole nation at a time. The ancient temple was local and aristocratic.

B—— showed us several old and well-preserved houses, such as the mansion of Assezat, built for Marguerite de Valois, the mansion of the Caryatides, built by Bachelier, under Francis I., with others of a very attractive character. The Renaissance style, the windows framed with fruit and flowers, naked children, satyrs and female forms, the savour of natural luxuriance, the taste for rich and vivid decoration, are extremely charming. That was the true age of artists; we are but commonplace archæologists. All our modern buildings, even the Rue de Richelieu itself, are vapid when compared with this—the Louvre and the Place de la Concorde mere scenes in an opera-house!

These mansions are terraced in front, with lawns, vines, and creepers, drooping in places from the height of the first storey. There are heads and life-like forms above the doors, and in the angles of the buildings; the fronts are animated; there is no allegorical and pedantic philosophy, as in our day. Renaissance folk loved to see handsome living beings; they felt the joy of life.

B—— took us to his house, and showed us his museum. There was much taste, with many examples; amongst other things a collection of weights from Southern lands, necklaces and ornaments of the Gallo-Roman age, and amber of many varieties. He has an enthusiasm for twelfth and thirteenth century art. He showed us some splendid tombs of abbés, with recumbent figures and grandly simple heads and draperies. In his house was a Virgin, a coarse, vulgar peasant girl, but yet a virgin, with arms too slender, and gracefully-folded vesture. There was also an ivory of the eleventh century—in the centre a Christ, and sacred figures on either side; a stiff, hieratic production, contemporaneous with the massacres and the brilliance of the first crusade. Each of these possessions has its distinct history. B——'s passion for archæology has stood him in good stead, physically and morally, saving him from weariness and triviality, and preserving his breadth of mind and refinement. His solicitude, his ever-present ideal, his watchful tact, have turned him into a Parisian.

FROM TOULOUSE TO CETTE.

ANOTHER wide plain, as between Toulouse and Bordeaux.

First maize, then vines. The maize glistens in the sunshine, a deep reddish or yellow colour. Each ear is in a dry or parched sheath, and the effect is a strange one. The aspect of a field is far more *granulous* than that of a wheat-field. The vines grow along the ground; there are no props, for the plant is in its native country, and looks for no support. The leaves are very green, and full of sap, which makes them beautiful under such a sun.

The buildings are square; in many cases there are quadrangular towers, as in the Italian mills. Many of the granges are open, and rest upon arches. On all sides you have the impression of a dry climate, and of life in the open air.

The towns extend right and left on the hillsides, Carcassonne, Castelnaudary, Narbonne, still half feudal and half Roman. Most of them stand on eminences;

with a view to defence. One retains its ramparts and its circle of towers, like a scene from Sicilian or Spanish opera. They are tawny and bronzed, speaking of an endless, age-long downpour of scorching rays. Eyes accustomed to the North scarcely know what to make of these stones planted on the rock.

As evening comes on, the bald mountains, undulating on either hand, and the old embrowned buildings, are full of grandeur in the bright purple of the setting sun, like so many spectres. On the right, behind these preliminary mountains, the Pyrenees stand out like white-robed virgins.

CETTE.

I CLIMBED the hill of Saint Clair. It is a veritable southern landscape; a rugged stretch of land, strewn with half-buried boulders, and intersected by long dry walls of piled stones; nothing but stone and heaped stones, all at hazard and neglected. Within the enclosures there are terraced gardens, with the red and gold foliage of a vine, or the heavy indented fig-leaves squatting on the low walls, or crowding pines, which emit their aromatic odour under the burning sun.

Suddenly, from the height on which I stand, the glorious azure sea unrolls itself—a soft and tender azure, virginal as the dawn. The mists are invisible, yet mists there are, though so delicately transparent is the veil that it can only be detected where the sky-line melts into the horizon. The rising sun pours a flood of rustling, tremulous gold on the blue silk of the motionless water. All is tender azure, the boundless sea, the wide expanse of heaven.

The grey boats move athwart it imperceptibly, like sea-mews in the distance.

The descent is by a long and tortuous lane, in which the piles of brown and ruddy stones are further reddened by the sun. It is a Calvary, marked out into stations. The extreme dryness produces no sense of repulsion. The long lines of wall seem to cut out patches of brilliant sky, and all the instincts of the artist are strong within us as we look. In the distance below, the country-side is broken up by long high ranges of undulating, misty hills, softened off in the background, and, though still more or less arid, infinitely beautiful. Their grand shapes, bathed in air and light, stretch themselves out so peacefully and magnificently! Round their base the marsh of Thau, a little sea left behind by the ocean, shines like a mirror of polished steel. Its splendour leaps to the eye, and makes a contrast with the soft aspect of the mountains. How the nobility of beauty is borne in upon one here, and what an earthly Paradise the South opens up for such as can comprehend it!

The flowers have a strange, intoxicating perfume; the fruits are luscious, and the enormous grapes are golden in hue and velvety to the touch. They are so abundant that the poorest child in the streets has as many as he can carry. Every man must have his vine, as the Italians used to say in the sixteenth century—his vine, and pictures, and all the arts for his voluptuous handmaids!

We sat on masses of rock, by a cleft half-way up the hillside. I was alone there for half an hour, and experienced the most keen and absolute sensation of happiness that I had known for a long time. The vast ocean in front was divinely blue, so that the sky was all but white by comparison. That sea is calm as Paradise; only on that wide sparkling sheet, whereon the sun shed his flaming glory, there lay a tiny fretwork, made up of myriads of almost imperceptible scales of gold, as it were a beautiful, happy, divine leviathan, cradled in azure. Two or three streaks of paler blue marked the sudden steeps of the ocean bed; the veined sea and sky were like the lustrous marbled valves of a pearly shell.

Nearer at hand lies the harbour. Some thirty little vessels creep slowly inward to the harbour-mouth; the three jetties extend their narrow, black stages in sharp relief; the lighthouse stands out clear against the sky; a dark old fort rises from a ridge on the right. These well-defined outlines, this wonderful contrast of clear and luminous hues with rough-hewn shapes, furnish a totally unexpected pleasure. The sheltered harbour itself glistens like a diamond cup. In such a land as this, it is easy to understand the origin of painting.

All down the hillside the ruddy paths diverge and wind about. Looking backward, one beholds the rough scarp of the tawny arid mountain; and in the far distance, the Pyrenean chain, half blue, half golden, swims in its pale violet haze across the fresh and motionless azure.

It is all an effect of climate; humanity can but reproduce and concentrate the nature that environs him. You can readily understand that men with such surroundings cannot have the same soul as the Northern races.

As we enter the town again, there is an air of neglect and uncleanness. The first streets are full of warehouses; the children are dirty and barefooted. The town extends along its canal like a petty Venice; like Venice it is built upon lagoons, between a vast stretch of inland sea and the ocean. It is an emporium of southern wines, with tuns and hogsheads on every hand.

The grandest spectacles are those which are unforeseen. What a vision meets the sight as one arrives by night in this unknown city, with sea and lake half defined in the dubious twilight; and then, from the roof of the diligence, these murky canals, these dark and silent streets with here and there a flickering lamp, the harbour, and, beyond it, the vast, immeasurable, unbounded blackness, a file of ships with their rigging and masts, like the web of a monster spider; in the midst of them a tug, black and grim, puffing slowly past with raucous breath, with no apparent object, showing a red and threatening light, like the one red eye of the infernal deity; and, above it all, the shrouded squadron of the silent stars!

FROM CETTE TO MARSEILLES.

FOR the first few leagues the line passes along a narrow girdle of sand, between the great lake and the sea. The water advances to within ten feet of the wheels, on a bottom of bright sand. It is of a clear brown colour, six inches in depth, and is covered with dimples. I am never tired of looking at water.

The sea is blue—a happy, smiling nymph—a Venus undefiled. The sky is white, with sparkling and streaming light. All the most beautiful notions of the Greeks recur to the mind—the weddings of the gods; their limbs of marble couched among the reeds; the waves kissing the feet of the goddesses with their foam.

The slender, quivering tamarisks begin to line the route; on the horizon one sees the splendid mountains in the violet distance. All around us spring the sterile flowers, children of the sea and sand; the sea itself, beneath us on the right, is like a vast furrow of pale velvet. Then come the vines, reaching to the water's edge. Lovely and fertile is the well-tilled land, which yields its fruit up to the limits of the waves. Those wide plains are magnificently verdant; no plant but the vine could grow so fresh and luxuriantly under such a sun. The black grapes hang in clusters; the husbandmen with their movable vats are half buried in the foliage.

The country rises towards Frontignan, Lunel, and Montpellier. The land is a veritable garden of vines intersected by almond and peach groves, and every now and then we dash past a pretty little country house. . . . What a land of vines is France! No country has so many, or has them so good. An attempt was made to transport a hundred vineyardmen, with French vines, to the south of Russia; but the flavour could not survive. . . . Our staple is bread and wine; in England it is milk and flesh. . . . Assuredly, the vine goes a long way to account for our temperament and our character.

As we approached Nîmes, the olives come into sight, and the landscape has a drier and whitened aspect. The rows of olive-trees cover it with their pale and gloomy foliage. There is a certain melancholy in their short, stumpy, stunted appearance.

The country falls away again, and we are in the characteristic Provençal land. First we have the Crau, a wide and barren plain, strewn with boulders; then broken and lumpy mountains, either bare or sparsely clad with a darkening green, low growths of stunted pines, heaths, abundance of lichen; all parched by a fierce sun; not so much as a spring or a streak of water; bare masses of round, whitish, coagulated rocks, of which the mountains are composed. The only trees are in the sheltered hollows, or on the lower slopes, and there are rows of puny olives and almond-trees. Yet they yield good produce, in spite of the risk of occasional frost. A hectare of olives is worth five thousand francs.

We reach, at length, the lake of Berre, which is quite an inland sea. I cannot say how many leagues it extends, but we had it on our right for more than half-an-hour. I should never weary of describing this wonderful blue stretch of motionless water, in its white mountain basin.

There was a black tunnel, more than three miles long, and then, on a sudden, the open sea. It was Marseilles and its rocky coast. I could not refrain from an exclamation at its beauty. It was like an immense lake, unlimited towards the right, sparkling and peaceful; and its brilliant hue had all the delicacy of a lovely violet or full-blown periwinkle. The outstretched mountains seemed to be clad with angelic splendour, so indwelling was their light, so like a garment was that light upon them, girdled round with air and distance. The richest beauties of an exotic, the pearly veins of an orchid, the pale velvet fringing the wings of a butterfly, is not more soft and brilliant. To find a fit comparison, one must look amongst the finest productions of art and nature; silken folds gleaming with light, embroideries upon a watered silk, carmine cheeks glowing behind a veil; and as for that sun in its splendour, pouring from its focus a stream of gold across the sea, nothing on earth could interpret or picture it.

MARSEILLES.

I saw my friend P—— in the evening, and his handsome, admirable wife. They have been living here four years.

Their impression is that the Marseillais are a rude folk. The first time they went to the public gardens, they mistook all the ladies for *lorettes*. So did I, yesterday. They parade, show themselves off, and strike attitudes. Madame P—— tells me that she has met nearly all the carriage folk at the Receiver-General's, and at other houses, and that she does not know one woman of culture. They are extravagant in dress and in their parties; they all run into debt. The young men are all self-indulgent; they have little or no education; they dine freely, spend their evenings at the club, and talk frankly, in the presence of ladies, of the women they meet outside, without the slightest idea of shocking them. P—— assures me that nearly all the merchants have two establishments. They keep their mistresses in very good style. Their life is one round of stock-exchange, brokerage, deep speculation, and sensual enjoyment. Incessant business swallows up everything else. They buy ten thousand hides, five thousand kilos of pepper, and then proceed to sell them again.

There are only a dozen students in philosophy, though there are nine hundred students in college, about two hundred and fifty of them being in the commercial school. P—— has no private pupils, for he is the Professor of Philosophy.

Toulon is ten times better than Marseilles, because of the naval officers, who are well-bred, travelled men. Here all is sacrificed to enjoyment. A few retired magistrates devote themselves to the archæology of the neighbourhood.

There are a vast number of religious houses. We counted thirty large convents in the directory. Most of the young people, and all the rich, are educated there. At Toulouse, M. B—— reckoned that two-thirds of the French boys and girls are brought up by the priests.

Here, as elsewhere in the South, piety is all external. There was recently a procession to Nôtre Dame de la Garde. All the relics in the town were brought together; they are to remain here a year, and then they will be carried back. All the Penitent Brothers, the town clergy, the lay-brothers, in cassock and cowl, with their banners, candles, and what not, followed in long files. Doves were tied to the crosses, with their wings bound, but free to move their heads. For a moment, P—— said, there was a disposition to accept the moving necks as a miracle; but a wag remarked —" They will all have roast pigeon to-night"; and the jest spread rapidly through the crowd.

Everyone was smartly dressed; they gossiped, feasted, and paraded. At church they were perfectly at their ease. They attended, and followed the service, but on condition that it should be taken as an amusement. Throughout the South religion is an opera, addressed to the eye and the ear. See what Madame d'Aulnoy says in 1680 of the churches in Spain, with their playing fountains, aviaries, orange-trees, pictures, and the like.

Marseilles is a great, an enormous city, with 250,000 inhabitants; we are told that it will have half a million when the Suez Canal is finished. It grows daily; there is building and excavation everywhere. The hillsides are levelled; the docks are increased in number. I saw it four years ago, and scarcely recognise it. The transformation is like that of Paris. There are enormous mansions, with abundance of carving, all new and magnificent, with seven storeys, vaster and more splendid than in Paris. I have never seen the like out of London.

A canal has been made at a cost of forty millions

to bring in the waters of the Durance. All Marseilles is supplied by it, and it fertilises the plains through which it runs. It furnishes enough water to give each inhabitant three hundred litres a day—even when the half million is reached. It is brought into the houses, and flows in the gutters. Many streets are watered by it every day.

The Joliette harbour is magnificent, and the Port Napoléon is now being built. There are alleys of plane-trees throughout. I saw a large number of new country houses, along the banks, and on every eminence. Ten out of the forty thousand hectares of the Crau have been irrigated. Thanks to the Treaty of Commerce with England, the wines of Hérault were in such demand that the year's crop paid 50 per cent. on the capital invested in them.

It must be admitted that in this country there has been a sudden rise of public prosperity, which can only be compared with that of the Renaissance, or of the age of Colbert. This year, three thousand kilometres of railway have been built. The Emperor understands France and his generation better than any of his predecessors.

I have had two drives, one to the Catalans, and the other to the Joliette pier. This pier is constructed on a mass of enormous blocks, as big as a room, conglomerates of stones and cement, which were sunk freely, one upon another, so as to break the force of the waves by their irregular obstacle.

There is the old sensation in my soul. When I analyse it I discover that the cause of this extreme pleasure, this wholesome and quiet enjoyment, is the simplicity and the grandeur of the landscape. Like the Greek tragedy and sculpture, it is made up of two or three things, and no more. A stretch of violet and soft-coloured rocks on the right; in front of me another stretch, rough and dark in contrast with the setting sun; a level sea, bristling with tiny uniform ripples; a sapphire sky—the soul takes it in at once, and every element is grand.

The long line of the Lazaret rocks extends like a sharp, rough, broken spine, with points and angles as clear as a piece of architecture, black in the purple flame which kindles the out-lying mist. At my feet the blue waves sport and display themselves like fishes, rejoicing in the last rays of the sun.

But my best drive was that which I took yesterday morning, with P——, to Redon. Not the first part of it. He wished to show me the old town of Marseilles, the suburban houses, the "cabanons," the "grilladous." It was comical, yet frightful. The whole of Marseilles and its environs is made up of excrescences—bare, rough, jagged, constructed of the light-coloured, sharp-edged, cracking and crumbling stone, a jumble of walls and little villas blistered by the sun. It is like a patch of leprosy on the town; nothing could be more ugly and wearisome. You might imagine that you were gazing over a bed of broken bottles, stuck thick with potsherds. There are all sorts of ramshackle erections, with linen hung up to dry, pot-houses, walls of loose stones without mortar, and now and then a wretched olive-tree. These good folk are content with sun and air; they do not ask for trees.

As one drives on, however, gardens and pine-trees make their appearance. M. Talabot has had 600,000 cartloads of soil brought over from Sicily, to cover a hill slope which he is cultivating. Waste water from the canal provides him with a good cascade. We sat on the overhanging rocks, which are broken to suit the owner's taste, and of course white; but it is the white of marble, in harmony with the sun. A succulent plant of some sort grows in the crevices, and the bees were humming all around. The sea laps the beach, or softly drags the rounded shingle. It is so transparent, you can see to a depth of three feet; the crystal waters of the Pyrenees are not more clear. The ripples in the water make a kind of golden trellis in the sunshine, and under this heaving topaz the level sand and green-brown sea-weeds have a lovely appearance.

I cannot describe the beauty of that illimitable azure, which sinks into the distance on every side. What a contrast to the dangerous and sinister mid-ocean! This sea is a beautiful and happy girl, dressed in her new gown of glistening silk. It is blue upon blue, glowing deep and far without an horizon. By way of contrast the long band of Lazaret rocks and the Chateau d'If are exquisite in their whiteness. White and blue are the virgin colours. How can one convey the idea of a colour? how show in words that white and blue are things essentially divine? In the whole landscape there is nothing but this. All Nature is reduced to it—a chalice of white marble, brimming with azure.

Far to the right and the left, the high cleft rocks, broken with ravines, draw the humid air about them, and seem to slumber beneath a veil.

We bathed in the buoyant sea, on a bottom of level sand. The free movement of the limbs in the water made one think of the joys of the ancients. The sun was high and unclouded, but his heat was tempered by the breeze and the cool water. Swimming on my back, I saw the coast-line, the sands, the quivering tamarisks, the pinewoods breathing out their aroma in the heat; the blue waves rocked me in my cradle; I saw the rippling silver fringe with which they line the shore, the keen rays, the importunate vigour, the joyous calm of the magnificent sun. How he triumphs above us all! How he showers his myriad darts over this immeasurable tract! How these waves cast back his image, sparkling and shuddering under the rain of fire! Behold the Nereids and Apollo! The Galatea whom Raphael saw is indisputably true; the horns of the Tritons resound in our ears. And those fair locks, those white bodies washed in the spray, would have shown up well against the azure.

We entered a seaside hotel, and rested for an hour, stretched at ease on the terrace.... In the distance, and where the sea-weeds rise to the surface, the turquoise and sapphire blue turns to indigo. One rarely sees a colour so deep and solid, an effect so full and so strong, such a rich and powerful contrast between the clear white of the sharp-edged rocks and the deep blue which surrounds them. Three months of life on this coast would chase away all your sadness.

In the evening P—— took me to see the old quarter along the Canebière. It is the poor quarter, the quarter of the loose women and the sailors. There are a score of sloping streets, on a sort of quarried hillside, with muddy drains which splash you as you pass; and every street has twenty houses of ill fame. A pungent concentrated odour rises from heaps of filth; strange glimmers are cast upon the darkness of the close-built lanes. On either side, from every house, women with their hair let down, often with their necks and shoulders exposed, in gaudy attire, so far as it goes, sit chattering upon their steps, challenge you, hum tunes, or shout indecent words. Some of them are pretty, but most are coarse and flaunting. Crowds of working-men and sailors push and jostle all whom they meet. In the best hall in the place there is drinking, and smoking, and noise; it is a low and blackguardly pandemonium. I have seen nothing worse, except a few streets in Liverpool. But here, instead of a resigned or brutish poverty, you find the southern violence and energy, the vehement craving for enjoyment, the reaction of men who have been caged between-decks for three or six months. A few deserted, silent streets, without an open door, with a single flickering lamp at one end, and gutters full of creeping mire, are tomb-like in their livid shade and absence of movement. You might take them for a horrid picture, drawn by Doré, of the morrow of a mediæval plague.

I saw this quarter again by daylight. It is a maze of lanes, inaccessible for carriages, which rise by irregular steps. Poultry and goats roam about them at liberty. The population, especially the women, sit at their doors, living a life in the open air, without any regard for cleanliness. An indescribable, pungent odour pervades every corner. Nowadays there are fountains and watercourses; what must it have been when the town was not supplied with water? Even now, the more secluded spots are infected. The water in the Canebière is of an extraordinary colour; it is a reservoir of diluted filth.

I sat in an open space and took mental notes, so as to get a clear idea of the type, especially of the lower sort of girls. They are short and thick-set—in some cases there was not more than a foot between the waist and the back hair. They walk squarely and flat-footed. They have full breasts, and their necks are thick and short. The characteristic feature is the square Italian chin, clear-cut like that of the ancients, or that of Napoleon, standing well out from the neck, and set in strong muscles. The face is wide, the eyebrows easily knit, the brow somewhat high, the hair thick and close, the expression decided and menacing. You might take them for the daughters of Greek porters, and they are overflowing with energy. According to Madame P——, their boldness is remarkable. Even the youngest of them stare a lady who happens to be passing full in the face, appraising and criticising her without reserve. She complains of the rudeness of the people generally, even of well-dressed men, who stare at and ogle a woman—even accost and follow her—or block the pavement, forcing her into the gutter.

It is dear living here. My cab-driver tells me that a workman's unfurnished room, under the roof, costs him fifteen francs a month; but wages are fairly high. For instance, a carpenter earns seven francs a day; a mason four francs and a half; a foreman porter from thirty to fifty francs; a common porter with a badge, twelve francs. These, of course, are men with good characters. There are some fifteen or eighteen hundred persons who form the popular aristocracy. In 1848 they saved the city from being sacked by the Piedmontese workmen and the roughs who abound amongst them, having established a wholesome fear of their fists. A foreman porter, elected to the National Assembly in 1848, resigned his seat after three months, declaring that he would have no more to do with the spouters and intriguers who, according to him, lorded it in the Assembly.

FROM MARSEILLES TO LYONS.

At first, olives; then mulberries, conspicuously green and attractive, overshadowing the vines.

Presently, the Rhone, covered with mist and fog, walled in by bare and broken mountains, terribly ugly and heavy, without character or expression. They are the beginning of the Cevennes, too near to borrow a blue from the distance. One can distinguish miserable greenish patches, the beds of former torrents.

On the sandy plain, furrowed by inundations of the Rhone, gardens and osier-beds do their best to flourish. The mountains, after a time, become a trifle less bare; the vine, of the famous Hermitage growth, propped against low walls, begins to feather over the tops. On the right are the Dauphiné Alps, serrated, but not unlike a row of slate-coloured clouds.

The valley is too narrow, too much shut in, too much at the mercy of deluges and the flooding stream. Clouds began to thicken soon after we reached Tarascon; the sky was flecked with a grey and gloomy mist; the whole landscape changed to gloom; the Cevennes looked desolate and repelling. How lovely is the South by comparison with this! I mean the true South—that of Marseilles and of Italy—not that of Languedoc and Toulouse.

At length came Lyons, with its high and narrow streets in a fog. In the hotel where I put up, one could scarcely see to read at mid-day.

Lyons is depressing; it rains almost every day, and the sky is always veiled. My friends tell me that this is quite the rule. The town is at the confluence of two rivers, close to a mountain corridor, and looking towards the south. Hence the constant vapours.

High houses, with a great number of regular windows in narrow streets, the broad, vehement, restless Rhone, an ill-lighted city, so that the wide Place Bellecour is but dotted by the feeble gaslights, which flicker in the dark—all this in grim contrast with the glare and gaiety of Marseilles. Of all the towns of France which I know, there is none which shows a closer resemblance to London.

I visited the Croix Rousse. I never saw a steeper hill in any town. You have to walk in zigzags, as in mountain-climbing. Descending the Rue de la grande Côte, it is necessary to take very short steps, and to hold the body well back.

There are monstrous mills, gloomy and monotonous as barracks, from which the noise made by the mill hands is constantly heard. As a rule, employers and workmen are barely in touch; the men do their work at home. The raw material is brought to them, and they undertake to bring the woven silk at a given date. They are free and independent, making bargains on their own account, and competing amongst each other. The employer is not like our friends of Senones and Allevard, with a nursery of men whom it behoves him to look after in his own interests.[1] There is no accumulation of stock; as soon as orders fall off, the workman starves. His attitude towards his employer is hostile; when two men take to bargaining, the only question is which of the two will outwit the other. Bad blood is the consequence. There were insurrections in 1831 and 1835. There is a garrison here of 30,000 men.

Moreover, there is competition from England, which does its best to be a nursery of artisans, and

---

[1] This was written in 1863. A great improvement in the relation of capital and labour has taken place within the last twenty years, owing to the efforts of such men as Mangini and Aynard.

from Switzerland, which works cheaply. Here a workman earns from a shilling to five shillings, an average of two shillings and sixpence. The silk is brought to them; they steal a little of it, and damp the rest to make up the weight. There are as many as two hundred prosecutions for this in a year. The middlemen between the employers and the workmen often claim the daughters of the latter as the price of their favour.

I went into the workroom of a silk-weaver in order to ask my way. He was asleep over his work. It was a wretched, lean, sallow face, with a black tuft of beard, and washed-out eyes. Many of these workmen have to ply their task in unhealthy attitudes. They save nothing, and the intervals of idleness are terrible.

Seeing those enormous flights of steps, those gloomy streets of the Croix Rousse, that mechanic life, full of painful anxieties, one remembers that the reason of it all is that our wives may wear silk dresses. So much misery for so scanty a joy! This is what makes Socialists. On the other hand, it is to be remembered that the laws which regulate work are unchangeable; that if you raise wages and demand advances when there is no work, subjecting those who are rich to legislative restraint, then capital will be withdrawn, and will take to itself wings.

English workmen know that abundant capital, under competitive conditions, leads to an increase of wages, and that many rich mean fewer poor. But as soon as rich men multiply, their wives must have silk dresses, and each of them wants the finest. Hence such places as Croix Rousse.

Heinrich, a professor at Lyons, says that class animosity has been diminishing for twenty years past; that mutual aid societies have been founded; that in the country patriarchal manufactories, like that at Mulhouse, have been established; and that the grievances of labour have decreased.

He tells me that in this town there is only a small population of superior birth and breeding. They are exclusive and insignificant, seeing nobody, and spending the summer at Beaujolais. There are many who have made large fortunes in trade, some of them the grandchildren or great-grandchildren of weavers. Now these quickly-made fortunes are more uncommon. Society is for the most part somewhat exclusive. There are small groups, to which admission is not easy, but when you are admitted you become intimate.

There are two hundred and fifty students at the winter course of the Faculté, and about forty in summer. Townsfolk and even the magistrates come for amusement, but nobody takes notes or genuinely studies. Heinrich came from Germany, where he had experience of learned and substantial courses of lectures, such as that of the Professor of Ecclesiastical History at Munich, who lectures every morning, and takes two years to exhaust his subject. But this course is academic, and, as the students pay fees, they take care to bring away full note-books, like our students at the School of Medicine and the Polytechnic School.

Here also there is a vast number of convents and religious houses. You cannot cross a street without meeting a priest or a nun. D—— says that mysticism is natural to the Lyonnais; we have illustrations in Ballanche, Ampère, Laprade. This holds good for the working classes also; they are Lollards by constitution, mood, climate, resignation and melancholy.

There has been rain for several days, sometimes a downpour for six hours at a time. To-day the Rhone is swollen and muddy. It is quite formidable to look at, with its big waves which dash their foam against the trees. It seems that they often have such weather here.

It is not a well-favoured population. Goitres abound. The young officers tell me that the hair and the teeth fall early.

The sub-lieutenant who helped me in the gymnastic

inspection pressed me to dine at the boarding-house of the lieutenants and sub-lieutenants. They do not fare badly; it reminded me of our boarding-houses at Poitiers and Nevers. They have a narrow oblong hall, reached by a damp and gloomy staircase, and it has a single gas jet.

The young officers complain of their hard lot, though they have thirty francs a month as extra pay. It costs so much to live here! Without an allowance from home, they could not go to the café, or afford themselves any amusement. And you will find them at the café for a good half of the day. Government does what it can. Soldiers pay no toll at the bridges, they get their theatre tickets at half-price, and their railway tickets at a quarter of the regular price. Officers have a month's furlough every year, and from three to six months with their families every other year. They have on an average six years in each grade, but sometimes ten or twelve years as captain. My sub-lieutenant has waited five years for promotion, and is spoiling for a campaign in Poland.

No doubt the life has its drawbacks. Some of them are lieutenants at thirty-five or thirty-eight. I was told that one or two were in difficulties with their landlord, and certainly twenty-five francs a month is too much to pay for a single room—there is no margin for amusements. A colonel's income is about 6000 francs.

Many of these officers are coarse and rough; refinement and elegance are not encouraged by their mode of life. They are loud, boisterous, red-faced men, and their jests are not good to listen to. I took stock of them twice, for an hour together, in the café. They kill time as they best can, eating, playing dominoes, looking straight before them, leaning on their elbows, talking shop, reading stale news. My companion learns the oboe for something to do, but declares that he will never have the wind for it. They are in barracks every morning up to eleven o'clock. Not one of them has the courage to work, or to study on his own account; few are bold enough to mix in society. They are bored, they eat and drink, they put up with a life of solitude.

Their only consolation is that their neat, well-braced tunic and epaulettes earn for them a certain amount of consideration. The State can do no more for them: the expenditure on the army is already enormous. And it is clear that everybody cannot be a colonel. Here again we have the characteristic feature of democracy—the struggle for life, and devil take the hindmost!

I was taken to the barracks. The beds in the

dormitories are barely eighteen inches apart. Their kits are on a shelf above, and their guns upright against the wall. Each soldier has his blanket, changed once a month, and no other bedclothes. There is not enough air; it is like the prison at Poissy. They are their own cooks and maids-of-all-work. Half the price of their food is allowed to them, so that a soldier costs the State seven sous a day, in addition to his pay and his bread. His aggregate personal cost is 365 francs a year. It has been no easy problem to reduce the cost of 400,000 men to the lowest possible figure.

They have their school; almost all of them learn to read, write, and reckon; and there is more advanced teaching for the lower grades of officers. This is as it should be; our democracy has its good points, though the craze for regulation and system is mischievous. The schoolmaster admits that the men are too much worried, and crammed with technical terms. So it is at Saint-Cyr, at the Polytechnic School, and in the military college. The universal outcome of competition is a Code.

My companion is very cheery and obliging, and ready to take me everywhere. The churches of Lyons are ugly, the cathedral commonplace.

I took a trip on a river steamboat. Lyons is built on wet rocks, and is all barracks and mills.

The school is wretchedly dirty. Both hotels and private houses are distinguished by their damp and narrow passages. There are one or two fine streets, like the Rue de l'Impératrice. A good public garden in the English style, with a lake, has been laid out on the left bank of the Rhone.

There is nothing to do here, except to make money. The merchants spend their evenings at their club, or with a mistress when they are supposed to be at their club. Not one of these *lorettes* has a carriage; but they are treated daintily, and kept under lock and key. I was told by the officers that Lyons was one of the worst-managed towns of France. The working-classes furnish plenty of recruits.

I see that there may be one fault common to all my impressions—they are pessimistic. It might be better to see only the bright side, like Schiller and Goethe, tacitly contrasting our society with that of savages. It would be more encouraging and elevating.

FROM LYONS TO BESANÇON.

THERE has been excessive rain. All the rivers are either over their banks or up to the brim. The old idea returns to me, which formed itself in my mind after my visit to Hyères. Lyons is certainly the border town between the dry and the wet country —the most strangely marked contrast in nature. But to-day, at any rate, I have another sort of impression; the wet land makes me sad.

Little by little I slip back into the earlier mood. Those delicate living greens, those faint hues in the far-off landscape, so pale and diluted; that row of poplars, resigned and melancholy guardians of the land; the drenched impervious woods in the foreground, renew their significance in my mind. The earth has drunk: it can never be anything but green. Yet its beauty is that of a face streaming with tears.

The South bestows new health upon the mind; it is a strong and persistent tonic for the nerves. The very simplicity of sea and naked coast has a bracing effect. Here, we have only fine sensations, incomplete and uncertain. There is no grand combination. You can but fix your attention on a nook, on the fringe of a wood, a dell with a glistening rivulet, a bay of blue sky, crowning the hillside. It may be that the fragment is not essentially beautiful; all we can say is that it excites personal emotions, light as shadows, and as transient.

Soon after Dijon is passed, the land begins to undulate; then we reach the Jura Mountains—mountains which are green to their summits. The effect upon me now is peculiar: the clouds must be ever brooding over them, and steeping them with moisture. Here at any rate there is no hot, untempered sun! There is not a breath of air or an inch of soil which is not saturated,—and man is saturated with the rest.

At nightfall, under a clear and moonlit sky, there is nothing but immense, black, undulating shapes.

BESANÇON.

I DROVE to the chapel of Buis, a league from the town.

Vineyards everywhere. We are under a clement sky; but the Doubs is in flood over the narrow plain, and has drowned its eyots and its banks. One half of the Jura range extends before us in a curve. The mountains rise in two or three stages, the last of them marking out the horizon. But there is no parapet, no broken line sharply defined with a bold contour of rocks, as in the Alps or Pyrenees. Only the undulation of a chain of hills. Indeed, the effect is that of very lofty hills, green to the summit, and several of them covered with woods. These great green slopes extend to an extraordinary width, showing a broken surface, and lined in many directions by trees, which fringe the falling streams.

We walked for half an hour along a ridge, over a fine turf, amidst the thyme and junipers, by the side of a stunted wood, under a tepid sun, and a sky veiled in watery mist. In front of us were two charming mountains, wooded to their crests—two beautiful cones of dark green, springing up from the dull broad slopes of pasture-land, and contrasting their darkness with the paler verdure. The sky shines feebly above them, with the tender, timid smile of an autumn sky.

Every landscape has its divinity; we must fall back on the gods in order to find expression for the phenomena of nature. Back to the old world am I carried for the complete and true expression of the sensations which at such a moment as this re-echo through my soul. Here one craves for a primitive poet to call forth the goddess of these mountains, of this tender verdure, this inexhaustible freshness. I cannot express the grace of eternal youth of these verdant virgin pyramids, haunted by the forests alone, where nothing but the forest has lived since the first dawn of day.

The type of the women here is transformed together with the landscape. Cheeks of rosy bloom, gray-blue eyes, ever varying their light like the waters of the Doubs, a youthful vigour and somewhat timid grace, unknown to the children of the South. But we are not yet in Germany: the vivacity is greater if the candour is less.

The College is a fine building, with wide courts shaded by venerable trees. From the front steps we look upon a wooded mountain, standing out clear against the light. This was an old Jesuit property, which came to them from M. d'Ancier, through the goodwill of the heir-at-law.[1]

"Besançon," the Principal says, "is like a Capuchin friary. The cardinal-archbishop is more powerful here than the Emperor. Every nomination passes through his hands. During the elections a few days ago he sent home all the students in the seminary in order to confiscate the bad tickets, and to put good ones in their place. They came back in the evening with basketfuls of bad tickets. The préfet was almost out of his mind. All the great lawyers attached to the courts consult him about the careers of their sons.

"The College has two hundred boarders, recruited from the merchants and country residents. Two large religious houses compete with it, and take all the young men from the town. There is an exclusive nobility, even more haughty than they are at Dijon, who identify themselves with the clergy."

I am more and more convinced that there are only two parties in France, Clericals and Liberals. In Paris the distinction is less conspicuous, owing to the vehemence and variety of opinions; but it is evident

---

[1] See *Zur Ehre Gottes*, by Meissner: a Life of Everard.

that all that is most backward, provincial, inert, and self-interested, is under the thumb of the clergy.

A Christian Brother has to subscribe two hundred francs a year to the funds of his Order. They live in trios, at a village school, each receiving six hundred francs, in addition to furnished rooms, presents, and so forth. One of the three is a serving Brother. They have neither expenses nor pleasures, and they vie with each other in sending as much as possible to the funds. M. Rouland affirmed that in one year the Brothers had put by 800,000 francs, and that he had been obliged to agree to their purchasing estates. There is a Brother Philip at Toulouse, who is a sort of king in his way.

There is no boarding-school for girls here; nothing but convents and religious schools. The clergy have a hold upon half of the men through the women. When a young girl is rich, they try to lure her, and make her take the veil. And at eighteen the mind is so pliant, the head is so inflated! I have heard of a score of captured heiresses.

It is to be remembered that our attraction to ideas, our speculative zeal, our Parisian curiosity, our philosophy and liberalism, are confined to a few heads, for a few years at a time. All this interests us between nineteen and twenty-five. A certain number of eccentrics are bitten for the rest of their lives; but the others, who are the vast majority, suddenly fall back into a life of actualities. "My interest and special business," says the notary, the peasant, and the shopkeeper, "is to live, to make money, to put some of it by, to give my son a leg up in the world, to dress my wife, to buy a bit of land; consequently, I must make friends of the policemen and the priests, who protect all these interests against dangerous people, and dangerous doctrines. We must not create difficulties, and increase our burdens." The only opposition provoked by the clergy is that which is depicted in "Rouge et Noir." "If they spoil my business, or demand too much of my money for their charities; if they meddle too much in my family; if their aristocratic allies insult me too much, and keep all the good places for their own sons, then it will be another case of 1830."

I find here a great deal that is full of charm and attraction. The sky is clear, and the air is cold. In the morning, a delightful and wholesome freshness falls upon the old flat-tiled roofs—high roofs rising sheer into the fleckless azure. One could paint a dozen pictures in the streets. Thus, at the Faculté, I went frequently from the Examination Hall to look at the fine brown roof, against a background of fresh blue. The vines and the bindweed embower the porch, and hang in festoons over the massive, reddish stone. At the end of the street the mountain swims in a luminous mist, and the sky hangs like a white canopy above it.

Besançon is an old town, full of Spanish relics of the sixteenth and seventeenth centuries. Most of the buildings are of large stones, and masses of rock, firmly laid upon each other. Their solidity and durability are in pleasing contrast with our offhand erections in Paris, or with the factories of Lyons.

The palace of Cardinal Granvelle is a mansion of two floors, somewhat low, with a large inner court, and a gallery running round the four sides of the court, supported by arcades with very low, obtuse-angled arches. Such arches are not rare, and they have a strange effect. The windows of this palace are very fine; they are set in a carved stone cross, and surmounted by a cornice. Nothing could be more delightful and cheerful; it is Renaissance work. There are similar windows in many Besançon houses. A well-preserved turret may frequently be noticed, or a lancet-arched door. There is a house on the outskirts of the town, in perfect preservation, which carries us back to the heart of the Renaissance. It is small, but in excellent taste, finely proportioned, and with a lantern-roof, the general effect being very good. Some of the flights of steps are constructed of grooved slabs, laid face to face, as in the Luxembourg. Grilled windows with convex panes are common, and there are many with diamond panes, such as one would see in a Spanish convent.

The churches are ugly, after the seventeenth-century Jesuit fashion, with bracketed façades, crude and gilded monstrances, and staring columns inside.

There is a curious Town Hall, narrow and stunted, with low galleries, a remnant of cramped mediæval work. Two good paintings are preserved in the Cathedral—a St Sebastian of Fra Bartolommeo, and another Sebastian of Del Piombo. The archbishop himself was in his stall, officiating in his grand red pallium. He is a king here—all but a divinity.

A painter might spend two months in this town. There are quaint narrow streets, without windows, blind and dark in the evening, like streets in Spain. The high pointed roofs, black with smoke, and crowded with chimneys, look positively strenuous; and the medley of buildings and balconies in the old hovels that swarm about the river is sombre and peculiar. The sixteenth and seventeenth centuries have left many traces; and, not unnaturally, the minds of the inhabitants seem to belong to the same centuries.

I dined with Lieut.-Col. C—— and another officer. The colonel is sixty, and looks like forty-five. He lives on the mountain-side with his wife, interests himself in the schools for the sake of occupation, holds an examination once a week, and gives prizes. He is a fine fellow, sound in mind and body, well preserved by the country air and an abstemious life. We need such men in France. There are plenty of them in England.

FROM BESANÇON TO STRASBOURG.

The railway runs along the bank of a rapid mountain stream, through a narrow valley. It is finely constructed, and passes through a tunnel about every two hours.

The country is delightful; the fresh-looking wooded mountains never grow monotonous. Their shape constantly varies; there is a new aspect every quarter of an hour. They seem to me ever alive, presenting here a chest and there a spine, prone or upright, grave and noble in appearance.

At times the sun sheds a flood of brightness on the sparkling meadows, soft as velvet. This strange moist verdure, pale-hued and fitfully transparent, leaves a vague sense of sadness behind it. It is doomed to die and to be born again. The South is far more charged with happiness.

The plain begins, I think, near Mulhouse, a broad fertile plain, gloomy and water-logged. Tobacco and fodder-grass flourish here. I found them again beyond Strasbourg, as far as Saverne. The land is a vast kitchen-garden, like Flanders. Fresh from the South, one is struck by the heavy, coarse, and profitable fertility of the district. The Northern races think much of eating and gorging. It is manifest in all the types. What thick-headed clods the gendarmes are! What masses of flesh are the fat little red-faced sisters! They are coarsely and broadly built, as though they had been hewn out with a hatchet. The Framer of Humanity has made His wares in the rough. For a contrast we have only to look to the alert and slender Southerners of Toulouse, as trim as if they had come straight out of a bandbox.

But the dark Vosges Mountains, rising one above another, and the sinking sun, as it hurls its last handful of golden darts, are very fine.

STRASBOURG.

THERE is here an aspect of gloom, an entire lack of distinction. It is a town where no one feels the need of refinement and luxury. I am staying in the big Place Kléber, and its sole adornment is the statue of Kléber, surrounded by four gas-lamps. The four sides of the square consist of low houses, many made of wood and plaster, all essentially commonplace. Our hotel looks from the outside like an ordinary inn. The roofs are everywhere very long and steep, as is most convenient in countries liable to much rain and snow. They have several rows of windows and dormers—in some cases as many as four. These lofts are not all used for living purposes, but every mistress of a household likes to have her attic for washing, and thus each house has several storeys of attics.

I made acquaintance with many of the smaller streets, and found nothing but the houses of commonplace, uncultivated men, indifferent to outward show. They meet in the tap-rooms; almost everybody frequents these places in the evening, and there is a great deal of drinking. Nothing could look more sordid than these swarms of men, in blouse or black coat, of every condition of life, under the flickering gas, in a cloud of thick smoke, amidst a deafening babel of talk, as they spit, and smoke, and jostle each other, and drink, and derive what comfort they can from that steaming and malodorous atmosphere. Such as are more particular pick their way through this crowd, and penetrate to a room above. At the "John Cade," which is the most pretentious-looking café, in a large and lofty hall, which is probably a relic of some older building, there is no distinction between the blouse and the black coat.

A few isolated types and interiors cling to my memory. Why I should remember these types more than others I cannot say. In a restaurant where I dined, there was a pretty little waitress, simple and rosy-cheeked, who looked you full in the face with a frank and close scrutiny in her blue eyes. In another, the landlady, within a month of her time, moved grandly calm, unconscious and impressive amongst her guests. Imagine the commentaries on that text in a little Parisian restaurant.

I was both amused and saddened by one glimpse of home life. G—— is a lawyer, hard at work all day on his briefs; and in the evenings he plays the flute in a band of amateurs. That is his ideal side. For the rest, he lives in a wretched little house, down a half-deserted lane, with no light at the door or in the passage. A servant shouted to him in German, with the voice and laugh of a carter. There were five children, not too clean, a litter of disorder inside his room, a dozen different things that were not pleasant to look at. His wife is half ethereal angel, half maid-of-all-work. These are the sort of folk who will live, like my poor Parisian scholar, or like Jean Paul, in what is little better than a stable, and their souls will be lulled by science or music.

It is easy to see from the examinations that we are back in the North again. Many of the candidates looked as though they had been frozen. When a question was put to them, they would remain for a full minute before they answered it. One could see the clock within them slowly beginning to move, one wheel bit into the other, and at last, not without difficulty, it struck. They seemed, with their jerking speech, like bears ensconced in fat, almost insensible beneath this living wad.

There was an excellent captain in the Engineers who helped me with the gymnastic tests. He was not a smart man. He scarcely ventured to say, or said with many reservations, how many marks each candidate ought to have. His perceptive faculties were not brilliant, but, taking him altogether, he is an excellent fellow. He was a soldier, and learned mathematics, not with a view to promotion, but for a whim. His favourite subject is analytical geometry. He goes fishing every week, setting out as the gates are opened, and brings home big carp, which he presents to his friends. He keeps his son under his eye, declining to send him to La Flèche; he teaches him mathematics, and goes out with him on horseback.

"It is better to keep your children with you," he said, "for that strengthens the family ties." He visits the café regularly after breakfast. I saw him in his uniform, with new epaulettes and a cross. He has feet like an elephant; and I was struck by his cheerfulness and honest common sense.

It is odd to see the Strasbourg folk talking German at the café. Each one speaks in his turn, as long as he chooses: the rest wait till he has finished, without interrupting. Parisians would break in a score of times, for with us replies and contradictions are explosive, as anyone may see at Magny, or when we go to read the papers. The mood of these people prepares them for political assemblies and constitutional life. Philarète Chasles tells us that the German immigrants in the United States fall into line in the most natural manner.

PART II.

DOUAI.

ONE is very comfortable here. The cheerful morning light breaks in through the three large windows of my room. The high brown roofs and brick chimneys cut the limpid air and the pale blue sky. Everything is clean, and bright, and peaceful. Some little girls, in tightly-drawn white stockings, are crossing the square, leaning on the arms of their nurse; a mother follows with four more, like a fine hen proud of her chicks. A donkey trots quietly along, drawing a market-woman's vegetables, and she is as red as her own carrots. A hussar rides by on his horse. Workmen come next, smoking long pipes. The square is wide, open, clean, free from dust, or noise, or smells. How restful it is, after Paris!

Above all, how easily one begins to dream of peace and competence! If one had a house of one's own, a house of glazed bricks. . . . It should have wide windows, looking out on a line of poplars, and a stream close by, with well-gravelled banks, where one might walk every day at five in the afternoon. A nice, good-complexioned wife, not too lean, placid and shapely, unfolding like a tulip in a flower-pot, and never disturbing my calm. Servants should wait on us, without any fuss, punctual to a minute. They should not be scolded, they would never rob one; they should have plenty to eat, go to bed at nine, be quite contented with their lot. The master, too, should go to bed at nine, have a clean shirt every day, a little green carriage, a sanded cellar, full of old Burgundy; he should entertain his friends; his house and wearing linen should be got up to perfection; well-cut transparent wine-glasses, with fine stems, and of good patterns, soft-toned china and bright earthenware, should make my table shine. We should not pine for witty conversation; the dinner should be so good that it would be pleasure enough simply to eat it. Our children, chubby little girls with pink cheeks and great laughing fearless eyes, should come and kiss their parents at dessert. They should have a lump of sugar dipped in coffee, or in the little glass of Dutch curaçao; they should laugh honestly and gaily, yet look half ashamed of themselves, as they slipped the lump of sugar between their rosy lips! How happy we should be, without asking ourselves why!

Along the course of the Scarpe is a bank of earth to save the fields from being flooded. Standing upon it one can see the whole country-side, yellow with the ingathering of the harvest, and dotted with clumps of trees. Here and there is the red roof of a house, or a long black stack of coal. The tree-tops, the widespread harvest fields, float in a limpid haze, which is pierced by the sunbeams, until all nature is clothed in a soft, aerial, delicate garment. Thus nurtured, every living thing expands with softer and frailer tissues, and seems to swim in an element of imperishable happiness. There are no words to express the peaceful vision, the voluptuous tranquillity of the poplars, grouped at intervals in the liberal air, as far as the eye can reach. The leaves themselves are motionless, as though wrapped in sleep.

AMIENS.

I STOPPED at Amiens to see the Cathedral. The screens which cut off the side-chapels from the transept are very curious, reminding one of a dense interlacing forest, with the exaggeration which one finds in a mediæval picture of Doré's, yet without his boldness.

On the walls of the choir there is carved the story of St John Baptist. The executioner is a superb type of a sixteenth-century noble; an admirable head of the saint, with closed eyes. It is a profound realisation of death. The wealth of ideas, the impress of the artist's soul, the great variety of robes, architectural features, plants, and animals, all the rich treasure of the Renaissance is borne in upon us as we look. The bud is bursting into flower. It was covered with gold, many-hued, resplendent, all but dazzling. It had nothing of the ascetic. The naked Christ, newly baptized, is already statuesque. The hieratic style is passing into realism. It is interesting to see here the end of the Gothic, as it was at Solesmes to witness the renewal of the Pagan.

On the north side is the story of St Firmin. These tributes to patron saints are notable. Every city had its little special divinity, like the cities of Greece, only the Greek triumphant deity belongs to a city of conquering heroes; here the saint in tribulation is for a flock of oppressed victims.

But the Cathedral has nothing more striking than the two bronze tombs of the founders, Evrard de Fouilloy (1223) and Geoffroy d'Eu (1226). They bespeak a profound and admirable immobility; they will slumber thus to all eternity. Not a single idea is expressed in these heads; nothing could be more simple than the interpretation. This is why the convictions of men were more absolute in those days; humanity was simpler, and therefore stronger.

AN EXCURSION TO ST MALO.

IN the roadstead there are seven or eight small islands, occupied by ancient forts. They are rough, bare granite rocks, full of clefts and ravines, undermined on all sides by the violence of the sea, covered with a crust of shells, like the seeds of milfoil. Seaweeds cling to them, stretching out their supple stalks, and their bladders swollen by the ebb. The crust is thicker by the water's edge. Crust on crust, these myriads of swarming nations have covered the highest rocks from base to summit, on every chine and cliff. It crackles underfoot, and your hand breaks it off in flakes as you guide yourself along.

The sea has shattered and defaced the rocks; and they in their turn mangle and contort the sea. They break and split it in a hundred forms, force it into the tortuous clefts, making it leap their little dams, waste itself in the pools, and dash against the restraining dykes. Every corner has its vegetation and its haunting life; each is a sea in itself. The limpets have glued on their solid cones, the red starfish, planted in the narrow crevices, lazily stretch their rings of tentacles; the dark-blue mussels extend their colonies along the slopes, and life is so abundant that they are incrusted almost as soon as born with the white little shells that clothe the rock. In the still water of the creeks the long flexible seaweeds develop their growth. Close-packed swarms of accumulated shells occupy the deep hollows in a glistening mass. The transparent water covers its blue bed with a pale topaz tint; or, lapping the edges, it sprinkles the sea-moss every minute as with a jet of pearls; whilst, all round the island shore, it draws its girdle of fluttering lace. This soft white fringe appears more delicate still as the eye travels along the pile of wrinkled rocks, the perilous bristling peaks, the stern ruggedness of the bare granite. Further out to sea the broad belt of blue sways as far as the eye can reach, under a white and luminous sky. Ocean laughs in joy and peace. Here and there it heaves with an infinitude of little flashes, like quivering scales of gold. Amidst all this splendour the gray isles, the walls of gloomy granite, the two headlands of the coast, cut into and hollow out both the white and the blue.

POITIERS.

A dozen years ago I found this town so ugly, so uninhabitable! Now it amuses me. Perched on the hill-side, with its tortuous streets, its buildings of every age and description, strangely piled one above another, it might furnish a subject for a picture at every twenty steps.

It is extremely inhospitable and exclusive. Most of the principal houses stand by themselves, each in its own garden, with its outbuildings, shut in by high walls, with a frowning gate.

A friend of my people, M. N——, an avocat who aspires to be a magistrate, has paid me a visit at my hotel. He is thirty, but he looks forty. Except for a trip to Paris at rare intervals, he has never budged from Poitiers. He is rich, and his family own two or three estates. He is unmarried, and is a gentle creature, scrupulously polite, oppressively proper, with all the provincial's prudence and caution.

He took me to Blossac, the public park. It is a large area, planted close with tall trees, and from its terraces one can see the Clain, and the broad plain surrounding it. When I was there, at nine in the evening, the town looked like an enchanted city, the city of the Sleeping Beauty. There was a long street without a living soul, and with a single glimmering light at either end. All the shutters were closed and the blinds drawn; all was still; the great black piles had a sepulchral aspect in their quaint confusion. The high trees in the unillumined void rustled unseen; the sky, diamonded with stars, suggested strange forms in the vast darkness which hung in the air, or buried itself beneath the ridges. No deeper impression of solitude could be felt in a city suddenly struck with death, overtaken by a sudden pestilence, and deserted by its inhabitants. The semi-darkness of the park, and of the indistinct horizon, had a melancholy grandeur.

There are four or five distinct and exclusive social groups—the nobility, the magistracy, officials of lower rank, commerce, and trade. According to N——, there are people worth from sixteen to twenty-eight million francs. He named two of these millionaires who took an interest in learning and art; yet they never see the professors and learned men in the town. Professor B—— has from twenty to sixty persons at his lectures, but his is the largest class. C——, a professor of philosophy, has nearly as many. Most of them are students, and that keeps people in good society from going. However, according to B——, nobody works at the subject, or is able to keep abreast of it. In towns like Douai and Cannes there is a better state of things; people in society take their daughters, but then the lectures become merely pleasant and soothing, like a familiar conversation. Here Z—— created a scandal, and emptied his benches, by praising the Stoics in comparison with the Christians.

The former rector, M. K——, had been a vicar-general somewhere in the department of the Nord. As soon as he came here he was placed under an interdict; not an ecclesiastic would visit him—not even the humblest abbé. The university is the enemy, and a priest who is at the head of it goes over to the enemy.

The nobility keeps to itself. When I was there in 1852, a new préfet invited everybody, townsfolk and nobility, to a ball. There were at once two camps in the ball-room, with a wide gap between them; only a few of the boldest young people dared to establish communications. And the préfet did not repeat the experiment.

This is the home of the famous Monseigneur Pie, who discovered Gisquel the Zouave. He is all-powerful. He directed that B—— and his wife should be named from the pulpit, because they did not go to mass. Last year he received a free bequest of a quarter of a million francs, to be used at his discretion.

A special préfet, M. L——, a very able man, had to be sent here to counterbalance his influence; but at the end of three years he grew tired of it, and went away. Yet he had some effect. When he first came, knowing that the visits of the préfet to the aristocracy were not returned, he stayed at home, which was a novelty. Afterwards, however, he visited all the merchants, manufacturers, lawyers, and notaries, praised the practical, hard-working townspeople, and made sport of the idle and rusty nobles. He pleased those classes, entertained them at his house, gave parties, and was the means of others being given. There were two subscription balls, with seven hundred guests at each. The effect was remarkable. Up to that time, the Legitimists were always saying that trade depended on them, and that, if they were to stay at home, the production of articles of luxury would come to an end.

These aristocrats beget large families. I heard of

one which sat down twenty-three to table. None of these have any occupation or employment, for that would be derogatory. Every member of the family has a horse, which means a great expenditure and frequent embarrassment. There are only two or three families in the neighbourhood with an income of fifty or sixty thousand pounds. A good deal of stinginess is the consequence. B—— shoots with the Director of Taxes, and one day he unwittingly trespassed some fifty paces from his own grounds on the domain of a certain viscountess. He was not shooting, but carried his gun under his arm. He had simply wandered too far. A gamekeeper stopped him.

"I was not shooting," said he.

"You must tell that to the viscountess."

The Director was very crestfallen. He would not for anything have the case taken into court, on account of his position; so, on behalf of himself and B——, he went to see the viscountess. She received him in a lofty and magnificent panelled room, though the furniture was very old-fashioned. He made his explanation.

"That will be twenty francs for each of you," she said, holding out her hand for the money.

The nobility have ugly and gloomy mansions, with poor exteriors. Within, the rooms are very grand, and the gardens are as large as parks. With the thirty-eight closed convents, this gives the town a strange appearance. There are little rambling, precipitous streets, with old grass-grown pavements, lamps at considerable distances, which are extinguished at night, joyless gloom, a dreary solitude after eight in the evening, and often throughout the day; unoccupied houses on either side of the way, bulging out or collapsing inward; few windows—sometimes only one, as a sort of peep-hole; gates which look as though they had never turned on their hinges; moss growing between the stones; silence, and a vague suggestion of any number of decaying, cloistered lives.

When I was there the young men, in the absence of other amusements, led sordid, dissolute lives. In the afternoon they went to their café in the Place d'Armes, and spent their time in yawning, and setting their dogs at each other. Apparently they still go on doing the same thing. A young Legitimist recently got himself into trouble by a tipsy exploit. Having no money, he had to leave behind him, in pledge, a family ring with his crest upon it. Next day, the Police Commissioner, going his rounds, discovered the ring, and took it away, leaving his receipt for it. The young man's father came after it a few days later, and there was a stormy scene. He went to the Commissioner, who said:

"I acted, sir, in your own interest. They might have sold the ring, and it is an heirloom. I paid so much on your behalf. If you will repay me, and give me a written demand, I will restore your ring."

The other wrote out his demand, describing the ring, the place where it was left, the date, and so forth. The préfet preserved the precious sheet of paper in his portfolio; he had all sorts of similar documents in case of need.

For the rest, the young men are stupid boobies. Their conversation runs in this fashion:

"The snipe put in an appearance yesterday."

"So soon? Impossible!"

"I give you my word that I saw three last evening amongst the wild-duck."

"G——'s horse is the best trotter in the department."

"I'll back my bay against him."

And so forth.

The prevailing temperament is soft and sluggish; no one is energetic, or puts himself to trouble, or shows impatience. B——'s lectures are the best attended. One day, he was blamed for a lecture he gave on Greek philosophy. The Bishop complained; there was talk of his dismissal both in Paris and here; he was called upon to retract. He stood his ground, and had the best of the polemic. On the decisive day, when he had to lecture again, no one knew what would come of it, and whether he would not be ordered to make a public retractation; yet there was not a single additional person at his lecture.

This sort of moral sluggishness is stamped on the faces of the people. There are many peasant girls in the streets, with their tall white caps and stiff corsets, like mediæval women. They remind you of the fifteenth-century costumes under Charles VII. There is a strange immobility and openness in their placid features, and therewith a French grace, a piquancy, a quaint and voluptuous attraction in these long slender necks, these intelligent though sleepy heads. People talk familiarly to their servants, in the primitive fashion. As in Brittany, there is a separation of classes which has lasted for several centuries. Three-fourths of the great events in French history are due to this cause. There is no civilising influence to compare with a religion or political activity. In spite of the French Revolution, there are still two nations in France—the Gauls on one hand, and on the other the class of Latin officials and German aristocrats.

The consequence is that religion is all-powerful. There were thirty-eight religious houses in this town alone. The Jesuit College has seven hundred and fifty students. Everything is overborne by the influence of Monseigneur Pie. It is calculated that three hundred thousand people come every year to the shrine of Saint Radegonde. When her day comes round in August, the pilgrims are so many and so poor that they sleep in a sort of encampment outside the town. I have seen the tomb; it is in a pretty Gothic church of the twelfth century, by this time well sunk into the earth. At all the doors, and in all the neighbouring streets, there is a swarm of women, who surround and pester you with little medals at five sous, others at ten sous, and innumerable candles. Old beggars on the threshold beseech you for alms in a piteous, quavering voice. Within twenty minutes I saw a dozen people come in, all of the poorer class, the humbler townsfolk, and all carrying one or more little candles. The richer sort are not content with that; they have been into a shop hard by in order to provide themselves with a better assortment of tapers.

There are two relics, and the imprint of the foot of Christ, when He manifested Himself to the saint. The two images are coloured. I saw many sous and double sous, which had been dropped through the grating. I was told that a few sous were laid there every morning as a nest-egg. Beneath the church is a very low and dark crypt, a midnight of awful and gloomy darkness, under a depressed vault, with a few heavy arched windows. One has to feel one's way with one's hands, or set one's foot at a venture in the shades of this damp sepulchre. The tomb is a hollowed mass of stone, raised above the ground, dark and sombre, varied by rude carvings. It is almost invisible, being plunged into deeper darkness by contrast with the burning tapers. Votive offerings, fragments of images, and waxen limbs are placed amongst the candles; the warm smoke curls upward to the vault; the stifling smell of wax is mingled with that of the underground cell. It is quite a mediæval spectacle. This strong glare at the bottom of a sort of well, over the bones of a dead woman, is a Dantesque vision; it gets upon the nerves, in the tragic silence of this awful darkness. It is the mystic grave of a saint, who perceives, in her prison of damp earth, sown in corruption, and ringed round with worms, the dazzling brightness of the Saviour. With a three months' retreat, and a sanctuary like that, I would undertake to train women for visions and stigmata.

Madame B——, who took her children to the Stations of the Cross in Holy Week, had to bring one of them away, suffering from nervous attacks. When I was at Poitiers, a peasant woman, looking up from the sepulchre, saw Heaven opened, and Jesus Christ in His glory. That was held to be a miracle.

A leper woman was recently taken there; she remained for an hour during mass, grovelling under the shrine with heartrending cries. She fell into a sweat, and it was as cold there as in the cell below. She came out cured, and died three days later. A doctor who came to see her attributed the cure, with the subsequent death, to excessive reaction; but the miracle was none the less authentic, and the incredulity of the doctor brought him into trouble.

Madame C—— and Madame B—— are thorough Frenchwomen, hating to be bored, and yearning for Paris—the very opposite of Madame X—— at la Flèche. The latter came from Amiens, but has become Flemish—a calm, cool-blooded, common-sense, placid lady, wholly absorbed in her household and children.

Another curious type is the Principal of the College, a former usher, professor, vice-principal. In fact, he has been here for a quarter of a century, being a native of these parts, and married a wife here. He has just been decorated, because a pupil from the Lycée took first honours in the national competition. He has the figure and face of a retired haberdasher, a smart vendor of Rouen cottons, up to all the tricks of the trade, an attendant at mass, and a reader of the *Charivari*, bent on getting on, but keeping within the traces. His highest pleasure is to sit down with his family to a melon; he makes little fuss, but bears his joke patiently, never protesting; a man of routine by birth and disposition, with a discreet smile and spiritless eyes; squarely dressed in a good black coat, and standing squarely on his big feet—the most ordinary, serviceable, steady-going, commonplace man, as vulgar and clean as a new-swept pavement.

Here, as at la Flèche and everywhere else, people pick other to pieces. The official class live together like cats and dogs; for want of a wider outlook, the ordinary pricks and stings of humanity are turned into hard blows. I have heard intimate friends exchanging the most atrocious scandals. And to make their stories interesting they embroider them, exaggerate them, point them with witticisms. The harder you hit, the more you are amusing.

ARCACHON.

I LEFT Poitiers by an excursion train. There was an amazing crowd, especially of the humbler sort. Change is curiously indispensable to them. What a contrast is offered by our full, busy, varied life with the immobility of the Middle Age! The more one thinks of it, the more one sees how completely the ideas of humanity have been transformed. The deeper electric passions, which used to be so excessive and so persistent, are growing rare, if not impossible. Set your fifteenth-century weaver, in his cellar at Bruges, joining himself to the Lollards, by the side of the Breton peasant of to-day—himself sufficiently in contrast with the typical conscript.

In my carriage there are sundry female types. There is a mother doting on her boy, possibly because marriage has not satisfied her heart. She is spoiling him, calling him her jewel and her darling, stroking him with her hand, taking his hand in her lap, brooding over him still, though he must be eighteen. She has but one thought—to make him a gentleman, and to keep him by her side as long as possible. She wants him to study law for a year at Bordeaux; and, as for him, he wants Paris straight away, telling her that he must compete for the chief law prize in the Paris Faculty. He is a pallid, lymphatic gadabout, accustomed to flattery, responding with coolness to his mother's warmth, and brushing off her caresses like a troublesome insect. He is vexed at having left his glass behind; then he tells her how he tried an experiment with nitrate of silver on a chambermaid, to see if her skin would turn black. Ah!

By his side is a cousin of twenty-eight, poor, unmarried, to her own disgust, thinking much of her appearance, well able to talk, knowing how to turn a compliment, a woman of the world, unattached and very handsome, with a Greek chin, a straight well-shaped nose, fine black eyes with a fluid film of blue, white hands, trimmed nails—a splendid woman who has missed her chance. The further one advances towards the South, the more helpless a woman becomes through timidity, blushing modesty, delicate reserve. They are types of man.

Perhaps it is that woman, in the long run, is modelled upon the needs of man. In the North, and in the Germanic race, man must command, and knows how to do it; he needs domestic peace; and besides, he is cold by temperament. Thus, the influence of woman is less; she is compelled to yield more, and yields as she is compelled.

On the other hand, different virtues gain importance and predominance, according to considerations of climate and constitutions. Thus in the North you find cool reflection, common sense, all the habits of calculation and self-control which are necessary to the battle of life, all that naturally goes with a sluggish disposition and a cold temperament; and in the South a spirit of improvisation, daring, brilliancy, all that harmonises with a lively action and sensation. Now the woman's disposition adds to that of the man a higher degree of sensibility, improvisation, emotion, invention, and nervous craving. It follows that women fall lower and become more dependent in the North, where these qualities are less serviceable, and that they rise higher, to equality and even superiority, in the South, where these qualities are more serviceable. A Parisian woman, versed in intrigue or at home in the salons, to-day as under Louis XV., or one like Stendhal's Sanseverina[1] is the equal or the superior of any man. A woman in the North, on the other hand, would find herself out of her depth if she had to control fifty clerks, or if she had to face bankruptcy, or to

---

[1] In the *Chartreuse de Parme*.

argue about tariffs, taxes, political economy, or the like. Life and dispositions in the South take a more feminine aspect, and women are more at home, and exert their sway.

Arcachon is a comic-opera village, with its pier of red, yellow and green, roofs perked up like Chinese bells, a league of ground covered with three lines of cottages, painted châlets with balconies running round them, pointed pavilions, Gothic turrets, more roofs elaborate with painted wood. Amongst the pines, on the sandhills behind, are châlets of a better class. There is a vast number of restaurants, wooden palings, shops, all new and varnished, like a perpetual Asnières Fair. Land on the shore is worth fifteen francs a metre. Twenty years ago you could have had half the sea-front for 2000 francs.

I took a trip on a steamboat, which crossed the bay to Goulet. One soon forgets the human swarm, and thinks of nothing but water, sand, and sky. Right and left, to a great distance, almost out of sight on the limits of the horizon, the sandhills prolong their undulations, monotonously rounded, just as the wind and the waves have made them. They are constantly crumbling; in the protected spots it has been necessary to employ fir-wattles and clay to support them. All other sounds are silent; the imagination retains only that incessant murmur of falling, crumbling, accumulating sands. Their long ribs fringe the blue water with a sodden, staring white; they do not sparkle, but no finer setting could be found for the sea than this conspicuous white. The pine-forests undulate above the hills of sand. There is no other tree; nothing meets the eye but this green of the firs, as uncompromising as the whiteness of the sand. The living fringe of forest rises and falls, and in the background recedes incessantly, with many a sudden drop and crest, and many an irregular sky-line. A faint aromatic odour proceeds from this mass of verdure, and mingles with the briny breath of ocean. Meanwhile the grey-blue water, fringed here and there with silver, heaves within its girdle of white plains and green forests. The port is a fine natural harbour, in which tranquil barks may crowd together and be at rest from the violent billows. Every now and then a floating medusa sails past under its ample hood, and with a web of tentacles outspread, like enormous mushrooms tossed to and fro by the limpid water.

This is the spectacle witnessed by the first of human kind: a virgin soil; sand and sand again; pines and pines again; reeds, festoons of climbing plants from one resinous trunk to another; a land unbroken, a mere ocean deposit, clothed by a single species of plants; and beyond, the great sea, its mother, enfolding it in her arms, and the dazzling sky of luminous white, charging its veins with perfume and sap. All around are marshes, glistening patches of sand, now covered by the sea, now bare again, with never a sign of human life; a crude, naked work, rude primitive vegetation on the deserted bed of the primitive ocean. When the first voyagers came hither in their canoes they found, it may be, a few herons, a seagull, a hawk such as that which hovered a minute ago over the blue waves, amidst the splendour of the rays that diffuse themselves in the whiteness. They landed; their feet, like ours, sank into the beach; they heard the same sonorous chant of the pine summits; they felt the pine-needles crackling underfoot; wondered at the white soil which at every step breaks through the thin carpet of green; half shuddered at the strangely audible silence; paused before some enormous thunder-blasted pine, standing upright on a bare sandhill. The land has scarcely changed since they came; and it is a sight which soothes one after the vast, formal, subdivided kitchen-garden, with keepers perpetually on the watch, that extends all the way from Poitiers to Toulouse.

Yet, kitchen-garden as it was, it produced in me

last night a somewhat mad sensation. I was alone in my carriage for four hours, and watched the hedges, the trees, the vines, the crops, as they rushed past. The wheels rolled round incessantly, with a deep monotonous roar, like the prolonged droning of an organ. Every worldly idea, everything that was human and social, vanished away. I saw nothing but the sun and the earth, an adorned and laughing earth, wholly green, and with a verdure so diversified, so widespread, so exulting in the soft shower of warm caressing rays. The air was so pure, the light so amply spread, the country so full of bloom and happiness. At every oak, every chestnut that passed me by, each with its individual aspect and its little world of companions and neighbours, I was affected as at the meeting of a living creature. I felt inclined to cry aloud:

"It goes well with you. You are a beautiful mighty oak! You are strong; you rejoice in the luxuriance and splendour of your foliage."

Every birch and ash seemed to me like some delicate creature, some pensive woman whose thought no man had divined — that timid and gracious thought which reached my ear from the whispering and quivering of their slender boughs. There was a sweet dallying of trees in the shady dells, on the russet and violet carpet of heath, in the winding paths with the narrow ribbons of sand, on the banks of a little spring which darkened the soil amongst the boulders, and fell in a little cataract of sparkling drops. It was but a sudden idea, an unchecked fancy, a childish sport, the jest of an infant god laughing in reckless mood.

Out beyond this plain of green vineyards, or scattered trees which shone and sparkled in the sun, the blue-grey hills bore their forest to the limits of the sky, like a circle of ancestral growths, more dense and stern, yet rejoicing beneath their veil of gilded vapour. From the upper tiers of the amphitheatre they gazed down upon their children, upon their young and handsome posterity of cultured, fruitful growths, which mingled together, sorted themselves, divided into groups, each under its crown of flowers, with its cluster of grapes or its basket of fruit.

TOULOUSE.

PROVINCIAL life soon deteriorates the individual. What a change fifteen years of married life have made in Madame L——. She gets red after dinner; she has three chins; is fuller in her figure and deeper in complexion. And how she talks! Journalese about the selfish, grasping English who rob us of our colonies; satisfaction that her husband does not hunt, ride, or fish, and so put his life in danger; all the solicitude of a nurse for her children, with a nurse's grumbling over the slavery which it implies. She was full of her working routine, of desire to see her husband promoted, even if they had to live six years at Quimper or Draguignan. F—— was describing two houses which he visits. In one there are four daughters who make all their own clothes, even to their shoes, and he meets them at balls. In the other, the lady of the house has a taste for hats, and makes a dozen in the year for her friends as well as for herself. These are all society folk.

Englishmen are quite right when they say that

neither trade nor domestic cares are degrading in themselves, and that one may be high-minded and large-hearted over the mending of stockings or casting up of accounts. But it is the consequences, the slow results of such occupations, which imply deterioration. One ceases to read or to travel, shuts oneself up in a narrow circle, is afraid to take liberal views, thinks of nothing but the education and dowries of one's children. Leisure and independence are necessary to one's full development.

The more I see of France, the more she seems to have the constitution that suits her. Yesterday, in the *Revue Germanique*, Milsand was condemning the article in the Code which requires the consent of parents before marriage. Nobody seems to lay sufficient stress on the physiological difference between different races.

We are Gauls, needing to be brought into line, and we have our ideals of brilliant devotion and chivalrous courage. Alexandre Dumas saw and illustrated this disposition to perfection. To divert oneself, to gossip, to be social, to jest, see the play, make love to pretty women, to sup and laugh with one's mistress, to fight cheerfully and promptly, to be enthusiastic for a leader, or at any rate to obey him like a schoolmaster or policeman, to leave one's duty undone, or to do more than one's duty, to be prodigal, to sacrifice one's self in a glorious cause, or a cause which one's companions declare to be glorious, to make no difficulty about submitting to discipline and barrack-life—all this is characteristically French.

Yesterday I saw the recruits in their quarters. They are lively fine-looking fellows, fond of all kind of games; they climb ropes and swing on trapezes, they show each other a lead, they spring about like young dogs, or rabbits. The sergeants and the lieutenant are obeyed instantaneously, without servility or bad temper. The officer is their natural leader, respected and attended to on his own merits, without any difficulty. During one of our revolutions a little stripling from the Polytechnic School posted a gigantic porter or butcher on sentry duty, and gave him his watchword. "Right, Captain," said the giant to the dwarf, "your experience is good enough for me." It was the experience of one day; but the dwarf wore uniform and a sword. The caricature is apt enough.

From all that I can see of the army, its organisation is excellent. There is economy, regularity, foresight; there are stores and markets; each man is utilised according to his ability, one as a baker, another as a shoemaker, another as a cook; all are trained to honour and obedience; many learn to read, write, and sing; everyone goes in for gymnastics, for expeditions, for talking, and keeps body and mind active. It is, in short, a scheme of national education.

MONTPELLIER.

I CANNOT visit the Fabre Museum; the Curator is away.

I went through the old town. Like old Marseilles, or the towns of which one gets but a passing glance, such as Carcassonne, Béziers, Narbonne, Montpellier gives one the idea of being in another world. There are big stark buildings, almost without windows, grey and stained with age, and reddened by the sun, often surmounted by a tower as in Italy. There are narrow streets, or rather lanes, paved with rough stones, sharp as knife-blades, painful to walk upon; refuse of fruit and vegetables in the middle of the streets, dirty children. The finest houses have a forbidding aspect, close guarded and silent as cloisters; whilst the smallest, the shops and workmen's cottages, throw their doors wide open to admit the air, a sort of blue curtain taking the place of the door. Grim darkness meets the gaze wherever there is an opening. Saucepans, pots of every kind, tools, garments, a heap of baby-linen, are dimly visible. There is a woman washing her infant, whilst another stands mutely looking on. The sight is more Italian than French.

Some of the poorer women do not speak French, as I found by asking my way about. A few years ago, a young man of title assured me that, in 1789, in the house of the principal magistrate, his great-grandmother and most of the other ladies could only speak the *langue d'Oc*.

The people are very sing-song in their talk. You might take them for young Italians of a lighter type. You would hardly believe, to listen to them, that they were talking seriously; they are like a race of pretty babies. They display wonderful familiarity and audacity. Their twelfth-century civilisation was a medley of precocity, trickiness, and extravagance. One can easily understand how they received a discipline and masters from without. They skip about like perky sparrows, intrusive and rash, chattering, pecking, preening their feathers, sporting with each other, swaggering in and out of their cages. Like Italy, this is a played-out country, which lags behind the others, and will not come abreast of them again, save by foreign rule and civilisation.

Nowhere else is the genuine bold type of Frenchwoman, a chattering magpie, yet smart and shapely, with alert and rhythmical movements, seen to better advantage than here. I come to the same conclusion as before. In the South you must live sensuously, like a painter, love a dainty, well-dressed woman, a merry face under a dark veil of hair, a deep shade beneath a long grey wall that cuts sharp into the living blue, exquisite grapes that melt like honey in the mouth: but you must hide away all that is within you, all meditation, profound or tender.

Here the beggar eats his honey-grapes; every poor devil has his drink of pure, wholesome, unmixed wine, which pricks his soul but does not intoxicate him. That makes up for a good many things, and it serves to create an ideal. A Norwegian, a North Englander, does not know what this sensation means; in place of the luscious grape he has at best his beer, brandy and beef—all strong sensations, modes of filling and warmth. He has no notion of pleasure. Such little elementary difficulties amount to big ones in the end; the ideal is differentiated.

As soon as the Gauls had tasted their first grape, their first measure of wine, they swarmed away to Italy.

There is the same contrast between the two landscapes. Yesterday, as I came along from Cette, I watched the scene without intermission. The line crosses the lagoons, with the sea on the right, the broad salt marshes on our left, broken by sandbanks and pyramids of salt. These glaring white pyramids stand out against the blue background in extraordinary relief. All around, as far as the eye can see, the water heaves and swells, varying from red to reddish-brown, according to the depth of the underlying sand, and to brilliant blue at its deepest, shot with silver rays, spangled with a tinsel of gold. In the background is a long line of plain, or of gently rising heights, tawny or tinged with blue, fairly deep in tone, as rich as in Decamps; and in this vast obscure border there are little white specks of scattered houses. Further away still are the round backs of the hills, the curving saddle of pale violet, and the immeasurable sky, flecked with downy clouds beneath the afternoon sun. It is all on a grand scale; there are but three or four lines, all architectural in their effect. It is like an amphitheatre of Poussin, but there is colour and richness beyond the reach of Poussin.

Here one might return to the noble life of the ancients, here found a State that should plough the sea, or fight, or create an art. Whereas the little valleys and tilled fields of the North, the sheltered inland nooks, the orchards and corn-lands, are ideal homes for peasants and farmers.

It is the sea which ennobles everything. Between the line and the surf there was but the ancient foreshore, covered with prickly tamarisks and mauve-coloured heath, with yellow sand conspicuous here and there. At the limit of the foreshore, the rugged border-line cuts clear into a deep and sombre blue. It is She—blue as any grape on this cluster which hangs in the cooling breeze. The azure deepens, filling up a good half of the range of sight. The white sail of a fishing-smack floats alone, like a hollow shell; the eternal monotone of Ocean is borne upon the ear. Draw near and see the leaping silver foam. Above the intense blue the sky is transparently, superbly pale, and the stars are hurrying to light their lamps. There is not a living soul, nor a plant, nor any sign of the hand of man. There might be Nereids and Fauns dancing on the strand, as in the days when the world was young.

MARSEILLES.

The sea is virginal, blue under the pale blue of the sky, enclosed by a girdle of white rocks. Divine are its hues, so chaste and sparkling, so pure and luminous and lovely, a bride's trimmed robe of lustrous silk, a robe for the fairest of her sex. The rough zone of marble helps to bring out this exquisite tint; its vigorous white stands prominent against the glowing azure. Above, the grand dome of heaven, pale by its very brightness, illumines the whole amphitheatre.

The structure of the rock is an added beauty; it might be fragments of marble kneaded together under some enormous pressure. It is stratified in courses, like stages of half-ruined towers. Some are sloped, and remind one of the remains of marble palaces built by Roman Emperors or Babylonian Kings. The divergent lines, the innumerable fractures, the infinitely diverse angles of the slopes, catch the light, and relieve the bareness of the great white walls with fantastic arabesques. The very mountains look as though they had been broken by mighty blows, and their ridges and promontories, their haphazard-pointed indentations, their bristling spines and crests, throw so many separate shadows upon the luminous sky. All is full of life; the whole chain of mountains is peopled with form and colour.

In the east, on the horizon's edge, the outermost saddles, shrouded and immersed in imperceptible haze, are almost indistinguishable from the sky. Unless you fix your eyes upon them you cannot disentangle their shape, which seems to slip from sight like an over-delicate etching. And all is sinking into slumber, as the light fades down into a suffused tint of violet and rose.

The day before yesterday at sunset, yesterday from the barrack windows, the sea was like a polished mirror in a framework of ebony; the light flashed upon me as though it came from a shield of silver or steel. I saw the hulls of the far-off, motionless ships, for all the world as if they had been frozen where they stood. As the sun sank down, the horizon glowed and lightened like a topaz, or a precious gem of orange and red. Underneath that luminous yellow the eye dipped into sombre blue, and the mingling of hues was like an exquisite chord of sound. It was all splendour and happiness. There sprang up a caressing breeze, exquisitely sweet and cool. I was absorbed as I looked at the innumerable

MARSEILLES CATHEDRAL.

ripples, the heaving breasts of the waves, the insetting foamy billows that broke upon the shining beach with flash of silver and purpling tints.

In M. Talabot's park to-day, I spent a delightful half-hour, my soul transfused by the *Lotos Eaters* of Tennyson. In a hollow of the pine-woods, thick with aromatic odour, the light of heaven was toned down by the dull and feeble green of the fine needles. Its azure was inexpressibly soft, and the silent foot-paths glimmered white amidst the livid trunks.

Marseilles is monumental and grandiose; its life is fuller and more spacious than that of Paris. They have dug out and carried away more than one hill; their City Hall cost them twelve million francs; the Saint-Charles Barracks is a vast pile, surmounted by a dome and constructed with wings, whilst its carvings alone account for three hundred thousand francs. The Durance Canal is carried over an aqueduct more vast than any built by the Romans. It cost forty million francs; it supplies water to the whole city; it pours running streams of muddy water into every street along the hillsides. The plains on either side of it are green beneath a burning sun, after a rainless summer of four months; the Crau itself is becoming fertile. From the summit of the Canebière, which is flanked by enormous houses, a veritable fortress of architecture, one looks down upon a forest of masts. Two large harbours are being excavated on the right.

It is the most prosperous and magnificent of Latin cities. Nothing like it has been seen on the Mediterranean shores since the most famous days of Alexandria, Rome, or Carthage. It is a characteristic southern maritime city, such as the creations of the ancient colonies. It is a harbour closed in by naked rocks, which have neither natural water nor trees. There is nothing attractive but the sparkling blue sea, and the bold lines of mountains bathed in light.

The town itself is an ant-heap, full of bustle and cheerfulness, with superb showy mansions, resplendent cafés, lined with mirrors and paintings, silk dresses sweeping the dust in the streets, bold handsome women, full of pluck and pride, brightly painted luxurious carriages, drawn by dashing high-stepping horses. In the evening a close-packed noisy crowd collects in a score of broad promenades, bordered by rows of luxuriant plane-trees, amidst the lights and fountains, chatting and gesticulating, in and out of the shows, casinos, cafés chantants and open-air theatres. Display, gambling, and the society of women are the three ruling ideas of the good folk of Marseilles. I am told on all sides that they care for nothing but to make money and take their pleasure.

In the evening I spent half an hour in a music-hall. It is hung all over with mirrors, and its extravagant display and excess of brilliancy are by no means grateful. What a contrast they afford to the clubs in Belgium and the drinking saloons of Strasbourg! Here all is sacrificed to the Boulevard. The music is absolutely insipid, emphatic and insipid as the violet wine which is drunk at the bar—new songs, a sentimental ditty on the heroine of Vaucouleurs, commonplace love-scenes, with words and music on the same poor level of taste. What the people go to see are the showily but scantily dressed women. One of them, quite young, with a blue dress and a remarkable bodice, adorned with buttons like a hussar's jacket, had a great success. At every burst of applause she bowed low, so as to exhibit a very white bust. This is all purse-proud swagger; these are the joys of shopkeepers who have worked and made money all day out of flour and oil.

A striking feature in this part of the country is the dimness of the colours; the light is so strong that it deadens them. From my high-perched room this morning I gazed down on the pale red tiles of the roofs, looking as though they had been slowly and incompletely baked. The leaves of the plane-trees are covered with dust; in the country and the neighbouring towns, all the walls are dull and monotonous, as if they were caked with dust. At Aix, where I went this morning, everything is dulled to the sight; the city, like the district through which I had passed, was a patch of grey under a little flood of fire, beneath the monotony of an implacable blue. It is a strange city, dead or dying in its sluggard's sleep, full of old houses with grilled windows, solemn façades, broad stairs reckoned for presidential robes, banisters of wrought iron, and vast salons with ante-chambers, in which a crowd of lackeys used to loll at their ease.

I visited a former President, M. C——, who is deaf, but vivacious in body and mind. He is a Liberal, an admirer of the English, and a decided foe to Catholicism. His wife's family, one of the best in Marseilles, which once had an income of £200,000 a year, has been sucked dry, as he said, by the craft of the ecclesiastics, by donations, dowries given to daughters on entering a convent, and the like. His wife recently gave 50,000 francs towards building a church. When he retired, not knowing what to do, he spent his time on sheep-breeding, and brought himself to ruin.

M. Lerambert, examiner for the Naval School, who is, like me, on his tour of inspection, is also much struck by the predominance of the clergy. The priests are the true masters of the provinces. Druids under Cæsar, bishops under Clovis, Pepin, Hugh Capet, Louis the Fat, and afterwards so powerful under Louis XIV. and Napoleon, have always had France under their thumb. The lack of moral and intellectual initiative, the talent for administration and submission, the notion of order and unity—in short, the ideas of Bossuet—are Gallic, and, at the same time, Latin. M. Lerambert says that their pupils are entering the army and navy in continually larger numbers. There is no one to compete with them, for their education is not general for all alike, as ours in the Lycées, but suited to the needs of the individual. They make friends of their boys; the teachers, free from family cares, are governed by a feeling of corporate union; their thoughts and efforts are devoted to the success of their colleges; and having no domestic ties, they bestow their paternal tenderness and friendship on their pupils. Lamartine bears witness to their success, and compares their colleges with ours. Young men escape from their influence between the ages of twenty and thirty-five, thanks to Paris and the newspapers; but they return when they marry, and acquire property, and think about the bringing up of their children. Their wives also urge them to renew their allegiance. The priests are well aware that human affections, the reminiscences of childhood, and private interests, are stronger than abstract ideas. They know that the mood will change, and that a man will follow the course which leads him back into their arms. Even before this, he has belonged to them for half the interval; the minds which are faithful to abstract ideas are so few! And how few of the young officers read or think for themselves! One of these, whom I met here twelve months ago, and who spoke to me about Renan's book, had caught up the word "romance," which the priests have used in order to discredit it. Their family ties and connections restrain them.

"That would make trouble at home," said one. "I prefer not to read, to think of other things, to go into society and amuse myself."

PROVENCE.

This year I have seen Provence in a drought; it has not rained for four months.

It is an Italy, the sister of Greece and Spain, as was evident enough in the twelfth century, from its language, its genius, and its literature. The contrast begins at Lyons, with its green hues, its mist, its full or overflowing rivers, the rain which floods the streets, the factories full of steady, hard-working artisans, swarming as they do in London.

Apart from Marseilles and the sea, this Provence is a gloomy land; you might imagine it to be burnt up, worn out, gnawed to the bone by a civilisation which has fallen to decay. There are no trees except the occasional mulberries and sickly olives, amidst myriads of boulders, and bare, dried, whitened rocks. At times there is as much as a quarter of a league of naked and sterile land. On the horizon, the unclothed hills pile their rocky skeletons one above another. Man has devoured everything, until there is nothing left alive. Wretched thorny plants, hardy little bushes, cling together in the hollows or on the cliffs. There is not so much as soil—it has been scratched and scraped away; for, on the destruction of the forests, the streams were turned into torrents, and washed out their beds, carrying down with them all that could have supported life. There remains but the primitive bed-rock of the earth, and the terrible sun. Beyond Tarascon we find river-beds without a drop of water, vast tracts of pebbles and sand, over which there runs a bridge as a provision against the winter floods; and on the banks are towns, still partly Roman, which retain their columns, theatres, temples, circuses, showing occasional Roman stones in old erections of the feudal age, ancient carvings used as building stones; a sort of motley in which the old cloak of a ruined people contributes a rag to fill up a gap.

There have been two destructions here—of Rome the mighty, and of the young Provence.

But the heavens endure, and by night all is divine as in the early years. Between Marseilles and Aix I was alone at ten o'clock in the evening; and I saw on my right how the sea and sky seemed to grow into each other with a marvellous reinforcement, as if at sunset the land had passed into a sublime and unknown world. The whole vault was a soft blue of infinite sweetness, like a bridal couch of velvet. The moon rose, and her radiance created a tremulous column of light against the azure. The divine azure glowed as far as the eye could reach; and the rising moon set it daintily back, as though to picture the innermost curtained sanctity of a silent nuptial chamber.

Thereupon came to me certain wild ideas. A sort of Lucretian dialogue flashed through my brain; the converse of man with infinite nature, the drama of humanity, the heroic State besieged by the brute factors of the world, with the combatants renewed as fast as they fall, whilst the eternal tragedy of life is enacted amidst groans and cries of admiration. Once before, this year, I had the same sentiment at Florence.[1] This Humanity, our mother, who lives again in each of us, is a Niobe whose children are constantly falling under the arrows of invisible archers. The wounded sons and daughters fall back; their life ebbs away; the youngest are folded in their mother's robe; one, still living, stretches vain hands to the immortal assassins. She, cold and rigid, stands erect in her despair, and, raised for an instant above the feelings of her kind, sees with horror, and yet with awe, the dazzling, deadly cloud, the outstretched arms, the *inéluctable* arrows and implacable calm of the gods.

---

[1] "Voyage en Italie," vol. ii. 80.

BOURG EN BRESSE.

THE CHURCH OF BROU.

This church was built by Marguerite of Austria, the aunt of Charles V., to the memory of her husband, Philibert the Handsome (1506-1536). It is late Gothic.

A remarkably rich and elaborate rood-screen shuts in the choir, which is an inner and a second church, more sacred and richly adorned. There are admirable and wonderful dark-brown stalls; the walls are lined with statues of carved wood, with a long top-screen, which is a simple lacework of flowers—trefoils, thorns, little figures, leaves, interwoven stalks and buds—a marvellous efflorescence and expansion of growth. Words cannot express the richness, the entanglement, the infinite variety of form.

But the three most delightful and surprising things in this church are the tombs in the middle of the choir—of Marguerite of Burgundy, Philibert the Handsome, and Marguerite of Austria. Heads of monsters, heraldic shields, grape clusters, and arrangements of fruit and flowers, twining acanthus leaves, delicate little trefoils, pretty wreaths of ivy leaves and berries, charming details of miniature bell-turrets and Gothic domes surmounting the fine figures on the tombs, make up a marvellous prodigality of involved and exquisite shapes.

The moral significance of the figures is very striking. They are genuine fifteenth-century types, thoughtful and profound, taken from life in a moment of inspiration, before the paralysing effect produced by the revived Greek type, with its academic uniformity. The idea which they convey to us is that of the manifold infinitude of beauty.

There are as many types as there are situations to underlie them and intellects to comprehend them. For instance, the draped girl at the left corner of the tomb of Marguerite of Burgundy, tall, somewhat bowed, with long rolls of hair partly covering her cheeks, is resigned and delicate, with an air of sad amazement, and the profoundly pensive expression that one might see in a refined lady of our own day. Another, on one of the sides, has her foot on a howling monster. Her hair is loose and her hands are folded; she is older than the first, a strong and noble woman, self-collected and enduring.

The figures in the lower section of the tomb are little masterpieces. One of these, dressed in a tunic falling over a long pleated robe, with a large cap on her head, is somewhat heavy and phlegmatic in the Flemish style, yet very pleasing in her languid calm. By her side is a shrew of some five-and-thirty years, with pointed chin, dress cut square and low, and a long-peaked Norman hat. At one of the corners is a simple maiden, with a look of wonder in her face, delightful in her mediæval head-dress, with large bows on either side of her head. Another, with her head dressed in a similar manner, is the most original of all, with dainty chin, well-cut lips, and the expression of a lady receiving her guests. They are all in loose, admirably-flowing robes; and they look as if they were about to speak.

Philibert is recumbent on his tomb, in his ducal cloak and armour; there is a lion at his feet, and six lions surround him. Beneath this is his undraped form. It is all in white marble, a sculpture full of life. There is an effort at the ideal in the little angels; but the limbs are not natural, the heads are insipid, and the pose is not altogether happy. It is the same with the ponderous and solid Marguerite of Austria: it is a conventional royalty lying in state. But beneath her shrouded form, the head representing her as a young woman, and her splendid waving hair, are fine enough.

In the chapel on the left the carved figures are

much ruder and more awkward, though they have plenty of life, sincerity, and expression, as, for instance, in the salutation of the old Elizabeth. In the centre is an Assumption of the Virgin, with the Eternal Father, and a choir of angels. It has all the triumphant effect of an Alleluia, a Glory to God, chanted in harmony by a thousand happy voices.

Multiplicity of forms and characters is characteristic of mediæval art. The impression is that of a complete dramatic scene, of a world in detail. The lofty art of Greece, on the other hand, limits itself to one or two figures.

How I should have liked to see this spontaneous Gothic art of the fifteenth century, of Van Eyck, Memling, and the sculptors of Strasbourg and Italy, developed apart from the imported Greek ideal and the academic pedantry! It would have been more apposite, refined, and vital; we should then have had our Shakspeares in sculpture, architecture, and painting.

BESANÇON.

EVERYTHING is green—the long lines of wooded hills which follow the course of the river, the mountains behind them, with their bold, steep outlines, and lifting their pyramidal masses into the sky, and the narrow strip of flat meadow-land on either bank. It is a verdurous vale traversed by a blue stream broken by the wind into waves of emerald-grey. The sun is low, and though there is laughter on the waving forest-tops, crowned with cheerful light, the deep interiors of the broken rock are still immersed in dark shadow. Here and there, beneath a white perpendicular cliff, like a wall of marble, rests a long black patch of light, three hundred feet from the ground, and extending for a quarter of a league. A luminous mist, a sprinkling of vapour, a pale, picturesque, transparent fog slumbers over all these grand forms, and the verdure, more or less toned with blue, seems to rest beneath a veil, ever deepening with the distance.

In the South, men do not get the idea of this virgin

delicacy and universal freshness. Here there is nothing which does not smile and grow; and in the heart of this luxuriant vegetation the river, fed by many springs, flows on in successive bright reaches in its many-coloured bed, all clothed in blue, and embroidered with spangles of gold.

At Besançon there are sixteen thousand men and women engaged in watch-making, and the number continually increases. They earn from three to five francs a day, but sometimes as many as fifteen. A family of eight earns between thirty and forty francs. Last year the town produced 311,000 watches. Many of them come from Geneva, and are Protestants. There is a Liberal anti-Catholic feeling which makes itself felt; some municipal councils have been turned out as being too clerical. The Principal of our College more than holds his own against the ecclesiastical establishments; but this is only in the North-east, and nowhere else in France.

All these Northern landscapes are marked by too crude a green; but the monotonous colour is toned down a little by the wandering white mists and the blues of the horizon. One thinks by contrast of the roseate, violet, iridescent, golden-yellow mountains of the South. There is not much here for the artist who has an eye for colour; these scenes appeal more to the man of thought than to a natural sensibility. The landscape painter in the North is compelled to modify or transform the greens, to wait for the autumn reds, the greys of dawn, the orange or sombre tints of evening. When he finds no natural harmony, he must draw one from the keyboard.

NANCY.

THIS is the finest and most pleasant French city which I have seen. There is nothing shoppy about it; I mean nothing of the smug and petty tradesman element. The prevailing fashion is that of the fine opulent citizenship of the eighteenth century, liberal and calm, with no sharp practices; resting on a basis of hereditary wealth, held in high esteem, with a certain position, magnificence, and art.

Even in the poorest streets, the medallions above the doors are marked by truth and expression, very different from the wretched Neo-Greek hackneyed style, with the inspiration of a *modiste*, which defaces the Rue de Rivoli. They are eighteenth-century heads, bright, cheerful, refined, often a trifle sensual, but always full of spirit and good humour.

These broad, regular streets, saved by their age from a stiff or conventional aspect; the fine square, so grand and pompous; the railings of wrought iron, picked out with leaves of gold; the roofs, edged with balustrades and surmounted by rows of braziers and statues; the street-vistas extending from the square without visible termination; the avenues of ancient trees, and the fine massive hills which surround the city, give it an appearance of grandeur, or, at least, of genuine dignity.

A portico, a colonnade, a palatial façade, when it has unity of idea, and is not a mere assemblage of separate notions, when it expresses the well-marked character of an age, lifts the soul at once above the platitude of ordinary life. A provincial town like this might well be a centre of influence, as Heidelberg, for instance, is.

Last night I saw the great church, with its two domes and richly decorated façade, handsome and attractive as the façade of an ancient mansion. It fills one with serious and lofty ideas; it makes one look on life as if it were a rich decoration, an embroidered velvet dress, that fits one well, and that one is glad to wear.

But the real masterpiece is the large and handsome public park, which is not too English, not too elaborately planned. I saw nothing of the suburbs. I had to keep close at my work, though occasionally between the various examinations I walked in the College quadrangle, resting my eyes upon the blue sky, between the falling yellow leaves.

The grass grows in the streets of Nancy. At eight

in the evening one makes out a light here and there, and all around is a deep inanimate shadow. It is a place not unlike Versailles, where one can live very comfortably with one's family. Perhaps, after all, our Parisian life is somewhat unnatural. It is, perhaps, a prolonged excess and enormity to live, as we do, on our brains, busy with literary schemes, with the occasional diversion of a dinner, an evening reception, a talk over our newspapers. But we cannot remodel ourselves after twenty years of that kind of life.

And here they are so bored; they long so much for Paris!

They print a Liberal Review at Nancy, called *Varia*. It has no subscribers. I am told that it is better known at Paris than here. At Metz, also, I was told by a bookseller that a book about Metz sold in Paris, whilst Metz itself purchased five copies! There are two or three Sanscrit scholars at Nancy. It is a forgotten oasis; but they correspond with other centres of learning in Europe. There is a fine library of 40,000 volumes, fairly representative, with modern books well up to date. The town gives 2000 francs a year to purchase books. The librarian has been here forty years, having come in 1824.

N——, a retired notary, who now dabbles in literature and philology, conducted me over the museum. There is an old staircase baluster, finely curved, with just the right amount of decoration. I think that in the olden time they understood the decoration of interiors better than that of exteriors. They cared more for pleasure in the house than for open air and ample space.

There are three or four things worth seeing in this museum, amongst a number of doubtful works and daubs. One of them is a fine Philippe de Champaigne. It seems to me that all these French painters are mere men of the studio, serious hard-working business men, and not pure and simple artists, like those of Italy. You may find the contrast in a grand severe picture of Secchi's, Pope Sixtus V., borne in his robes of ceremony by a dozen strong red-faced varlets wearing his livery. Here we have a free, broad artistic idea, a large detail of actual life, cut out and transferred to canvas, with no philosophy or antecedent theory, and speaking to the mind only through the eyes.

The gate from the ducal palace (fifteenth century) is charming; it is rich, decorated, original, and honest. The chapel containing their tombs is like an extinguisher, a sort of high conical chimney, in which two or three hundred mincing and insipid angels rise up into a pyramid, like so many rows of hams. The coffers containing the ashes resemble closed pepper-boxes, surmounted by a device like cross-bones from a frog. But on your left, as you enter, there is a rather fine figure of some Middle-Age duchess or other, white, wrinkled, recumbent on her tomb, covered with a dark mantle, and giving the impression of eternal rest.

At Metz the Jesuits have five hundred pupils. General de Martimprez changed the regular time for the military band in order that the pupils of the Jesuits might hear it; and so the pupils of the Lycée hear it no longer. The Jesuits have other great colleges at Paris, Vaugirard, Poitiers, Toulouse, Lyons, Amiens, and sundry smaller towns. The older Liberals, the magistrates, engineers, and military men, send their sons to them, because it is supposed to be the proper thing to do; because the food and general regulations are said to be superior; because boys make good acquaintances there, likely to be useful in the future. In this way an old pupil has just made a very good match. Other reasons which I heard were, that a boy's mother had worried to have him placed with the Jesuits until he had made his first communion, and then worried to have him let alone; and that the fathers make themselves the comrades of their pupils, whereas our professors are cold, and the teachers are supposed to be hostile.

At Nancy, which is a Liberal town, twenty-three town councillors out of twenty-nine, and three professors out of five, profess Catholic ideas. There are also many religious foundations, convents for girls, a college for law-students, and so on.

I had some talk with Madame de ——. Her sons are with the Jesuits at Metz. They are so successful that they have refused seventeen pupils this year. They captivate the mothers by making a display of maternity. "Do not be anxious about him," one of the professors said; "if he is all alone, then I will be his father," and he stroked the lad gently on the head. They win over the children and become their comrades, walking arm-in-arm with them in the quadrangles, out of school hours. The boys like them, and, when they grow up, come back to see them. There is no compulsory piety, but a pupil who did not receive the sacrament at Easter would be sent away. As a rule, there is confession once a month, and in this way the priests gain their confidence and know all their circumstances. Then again they confess in the town, and thus keep up a connection with the parents. They pay great attention to the food, dress, and manners of their pupils. In some of their establishments they provide dancing and riding masters; their aim is to turn out fine gentlemen. That is another hold upon the family, and especially upon the women.

A father was present at all our examinations, in order to hear the questions which we put, so as to prepare on the same lines for the subsequent year. Whenever a pupil passed his examination, his master was there to support him.

They send their weakest pupils to the provincial centres, reserving their brilliant ones for Paris, and they are wonderfully adroit in making the most of their materials. Thus gymnastics, though counting in the examinations, were found to be generally neglected. They immediately put on an excellent master, and made daily drill compulsory. In this subject, accordingly, their pupils were decidedly superior.

RHEIMS.

ONLY the porch of the Cathedral is fully exposed to view; the north face is partly exposed. The remainder is almost completely hidden by a heavy-looking episcopal palace of the eighteenth century, by lanes running close against the Cathedral walls, and by a monstrous new erection of stone, a long array of barbarous eye-sores. What a contrast with the noble epoch of the year 1200! That was a Homeric age.

Its fundamental idea was the parallel between the theology then taught by St Bernard, Albertus Magnus, and St Thomas Aquinas, the religion of prose, and architecture, which is the religion of the imaginative soul—both in the dawn of renaissance.

It is a pile absolutely out of the common; in richness and elegance far above the Cathedrals of Paris, Tours, and Strasbourg. It blossoms and flourishes like Danté's luxuriant tree of mystic flowers.

Its style is entirely lanceolate. The façade is like a carved reliquary, mystic, efflorescent, worthy to be of beaten gold. Now you could not imagine a golden Parthenon. There is no exaggeration, as at Milan. It is the fulfilment and the flower of the Gothic.

The apse is admirable, a masterpiece like that at Cologne, though distinct in feeling. How different from that paltry array of buttresses at Notre Dame, which remind one of a crab—a reminiscence of Saint Sernin, a sample of south-Italian!

There are evidently different periods in this Cathedral. Viollet-le-Duc says that in the fifteenth century the original design was always followed, but that after that century the work was shortened for want of money. And it is manifest from the patches of masonry, the iron clamps, and sundry restorations, that the edifice was frail. Gothic is always under repair.

I saw St Remy, the main part of which is only about half a century older than the Cathedral. The difference is enormous. The wide nave ends in a concave choir. There is breathing-space; it is strong, serene, and fine, in the antique fashion.

The white chalky soil of Champagne is horrible. It has an absolutely prosaic effect. There is not a refined shape or colour to be seen. Art will never flourish here: witness the inflamed eye, the cunning mouth, the jeering voice, the big, irregular, vulgar nose of the inhabitants.

The prevailing characteristic of French provincial life, such as our constitution makes it, is that men have no occupation. They begin with a keen scramble, and then grow torpid. It is a sort of animal hybernation.

France is, and will continue to be, a democracy, impelled by men who write, and controlled by officials. The influence of men of understanding is transient, and only skin-deep, for want of a stable proprietary class. Rural landowners have nothing to do but to look after their own possessions. Some few have an outlet in the Society of St Vincent de Paul; others lend books through the village libraries, and visit the schools. But they are not men of action; they have no true initiative. They fade out of sight, grow morose, and complain that the Government suppresses them; that they have nothing in which they can take a part, either individually or in association. They cannot start a new sect, or a political agitation. The sanction of the State was needed before the Society of St Vincent de Paul could be established, and it is purely charitable, with no other qualification than that of being a Catholic communicant.

The effect of provincial life is to attenuate the individual, to exhaust his faculties in little whims and trifling duties: for women, cookery, domestic arrangements, the kitchen-garden, the prevention of waste, the tending of flowers, the making of artificial flowers, crucifixes and boxes, paying calls, and gossiping like a revolving wheel, attending church and telling their beads; for men, the café, the club, the dinner of many courses. The main point is to kill time, whether your calling is to be a magistrate, to play cup and ball, or to whip a trout-stream. It is vocation enough to manage your property and husband your estate; you become a slave to your house or to your garden, and indulge yourself with a game of dominoes or a glass of beer at the café.

Religion owes much of its power in the country to the fact of its being an occupation, a mechanical exercise which gets through a certain number of hours; and the power of the clergy consists in their being a class of officials. As for mysticism, it is for a small number of sickly or select souls, one in thirty at the outside.

The state of France is like a state of siege; every moment the liberty of the individual is being sacrificed to the State.

In any true State, everything depends on the degree and kind of impression which the aggregate of individuals receive from any given event. An exacting and restrictive government becomes necessary amongst Frenchmen, with their excitability, their suspicious restlessness, their great foresight, their rapidity of logical reasoning. Witness the terror produced by Socialism in 1851, which made them throw themselves into the arms of a President.

On my return to Paris, I discussed all this with Hillebrand.[1] I maintained that the originative force of the Frenchman is not, as he said, vanity, but the necessity for excitement. A German can stand being bored, or put up with gloomy impressions, more easily than a Frenchman.

He holds that France is superior to Germany in its aptitude for association. She has an instinct, a tact, a talent for conversation and society, because she is impelled to talk, is naturally polite, has the desire to shine, the gift of self-adornment, an aptitude for expansion, a readiness in passing from one idea to another, and from one subject to another. More than that, she has public spirit, a faculty of unanimous

---

[1] Karl Hillebrand, author of "Frankreich und die Franzosen."

perception, of coalescence and combination on any particular question, and of immediate action upon it. Thus, there was a clear expression of this public spirit in 1788, in 1829, in June 1848, in December 1852. Men act together, when their ideas are few in number, simple, clear, and contagious; whilst the individualist German marches along on his own account, differing from all who surround him, and it is not easy to rouse him into action.

France has more traditions and codes of honour, politeness, and good breeding; every individual, like the aggregate, sets out with a moral judgment capable of being applied to all events of primary importance, and of telling him clearly what he ought to do and believe in particular cases. It is the same in England, thanks to the antiquity of their culture and political existence. Germany, on the other hand, is new, unsettled, irresolute.

PART III.

CALIFORNIA

THE BELFRY AT DOUAI.

DOUAI.

ONCE again the same impression of peace and comfort, of neatness and the picturesque. The walls are new painted, glazed, or whitened every year. The buildings and gardens, all that shows from without, are like smug and prudent citizens in their Sunday clothes.

But the effect of the place on the eyes is very fine. A grand moving mass of murky rain-clouds now and again reveals behind its gloomy hues a chink of delicious blue or fleecy white. Against this softened background you have the slated roofs, with their red chimney-stacks, the long white walls of glazed bricks, the groups of luxuriant poplars, the thousand trees and lawns of lovely green, the manifold verdure dishevelled by the buffeting mist-laden winds. And set within the cloudy mass is the belfry of the Palais de Justice, its turreted summit whimsically adorned with leaden caps and heraldic animals.

It is only in the lands of mist, where the dome

of the sky is half obliterated, that the hues of nature have their full effect. The red and green were an excellent contrast to the half-effaced and melting background.

The air was impregnated as it were with imperceptible vapour, and the moist warmth did not prevent the sky from being bright and soft. The broad garments of the poplars hung feebly swaying in the thin luminous mist. The tender well-nourished leaves were remarkably rich in hue and delicate in tissue. In the park yesterday I slept a balmy sleep, wrapped in the universal warmth and vital freshness of Nature. A tall pine, like those I have seen in Corsica, mounted upward like a tower, and its head swam in the diaphanous mist.

The houses please me very much. The roofs are especially striking, being very lofty, steep, solid-looking, with small red tiles that seem to be as thick as bricks, and form a strong shell to carry the snows of winter. The old brick chimneys rise casually from the roofs, mostly as a natural prolongation, well set on their bases, and not stuck on anyhow, as in the midland towns of France. The house is a complete body, with head and trunk. All these irregular horned heads lie in a broad fantastic strip across the cloudy sky.

I have an eye for Flemish types. I spent half

an hour in a little courtyard, behind the college, studying two or three lofty houses, capped with their high roofs and red chimneys; two or three more with slated roofs, and bricks of several colours, or shining with white paint—deep contrasted colours, strong and bright, set off by the intense green of the occasional poplars, steeped in the humid atmosphere, and girt round by the floating mist—charming woolly fleeces, a shifting veil of fog, banks of cloud and tattered bands of vapour, which rolls by or condenses as it falls amidst the slated house-tops. There are scores of such houses, on which one looks again and again, as though they were living faces, and which one would gladly paint. Nothing more is wanted; they would make an ample subject. Flemish pictures are just the same in feeling—very soft and very simple.

All over the place you see the servants washing and cleaning. The poorest of the people at least once a year, on the Fête de Gayant, cleanse their houses thoroughly, both inside and out. Householders find it advisable to engage the painters and white-washers six months beforehand.

Many of the gardens are large and very lovely, crowded with plants, which enliven with their green the red and the deep brown of the nearest houses the strange and well-marked shapes of the roofs. The silent, all but spotless streets refresh the sight, all streaked with red, white, and brown, as evenly as some piece of coloured cloth.

Bickering, backbiting, petty rivalries, indiscretions, scandal, and spying—there you have the flies, and wasps, and gadflies, which mar this scene of peace and comfort.

I spent a day at Lille. There is nothing to remark upon except the museum. It is a Flemish town, like Douai, but with less of repose, and less pure in style. Round about it, as about Douai, there spreads an endless plain, a great flat kitchen-garden, casually dotted with trees, yellow with bound sheaves, chequered with fields of flowering poppies and coarse-leaved beetroot, and low or pointed roofs. There are myriads of fields, richly nurtured by the low overhanging sky, with its lazy, slumbering clouds and riddled light, which oozes through the fleecy mist. White flocks of down dwindle and evaporate amongst the grey and black clouds, which fall now and again in streams or sheets of rain. The vapour incessantly rises from the soil, scatters, collects into a mass, until it falls again to fertilise the ever-teeming earth. The blended varying hue, the sun-pierced fog, the air thick with moist and melting vapours, lulled and rejoiced my eyes with their changing and softening tints; and, when the mist had fallen in rain, my soul was refreshed to see the dripping poplars shine and glisten again in the drying sun.

When I returned to Douai in the evening, all the townsfolk were out in the square in their Sunday best—neat white frocks and dainty bonnets. It was impossible to move about with freedom, or to find a chair; the crowd was as dense as at the Tuileries, or in the Champs Elysées, for to-day there was music in the square. To put on your best dress and listen to the brass band is the poetry of this life of domesticity, of perpetual cleanliness, and sluggish ease. It was the same round of domestic duties as I witnessed in the house of M. V——, near Mons. Twice or thrice in a day three little children were undressed and dressed again; there was a never-ending succession of needlewomen and washerwomen; nothing but wash-tubs and the overhauling of linen-chests. The husband's domain is his cellar, and he is as much devoted to it as if it were a library.

A blank day, except for a pleasant impression of the old province of Le Perche, and in the outskirts of Le Mans. The country is nothing but hills—green hills with little streams flowing between the alders, all pasture-land, and every meadow bordered by lines of forest trees—oaks and others. The oaks are of all ages and of every shape, spreading and upright, sometimes broken and squat, but inexpressibly verdant. For leagues at a time this verdure never ceases. The round luxuriant tree-tops succeed each other as far as the eye can reach; occasionally a grove of pines contributes its inexhaustible freshness. The ancient poetry of the virgin landscape is not yet absolutely extinct; man has not yet utterly consumed the primitive forest. He has saved the fringe, and the oaks are as free and as vital as in the freshness of dawn.

LA FLÈCHE.

IN the afternoon I was on board a steamboat on the Loir. On both sides of us all was green and crowded with vegetation. The river was full of aquatic plants, water-lilies, bulrushes, and tufted reeds; and the reeds, with their stiff flat leaves, were crowded together on the banks by tens of thousands, bending under their burden of red seeds.

To right and left nothing but meadows of thick grass, hedges of oaks and poplars—a great flat basin of verdure. The green river advances with a broad full stream, overflowing in little marshes or long backwaters, and irrigating the fertile soil. A grey sky, heavy with falling mist, hangs over the saturated land; the sifted light pours down upon a distant hedge and meadow-side, and a warm vapour floats incessantly between earth and sky. Sometimes in the horizon, between the still green summits of the poplars, a violet patch of sky, wellnigh black, throws out with greater vividness the young and freshly illuminated verdure. Then comes the shower. The river seems to boil beneath innumerable big drops of rain. The emptied cloud sheers off, and wandering white mists hang around the trees like a torn robe of muslin, until the strong sunlight awakens a glorious life in the grass, and the undergrowth sparkles with a stream of white pearls.

A couple of officers with whom I have been conversing told me that they could not afford to cling to their profession; it cost too much to live. There are plenty of sergeant-majors who could pass their examinations and become sub-lieutenants; but they say to the Inspector-General sometimes :—

"I might have worked at my books and become an officer. But I should have had to wait ten years, and my family is poor, and could not support me. I preferred to read the books in my leisure moments, but when I am out of my time I shall go into a merchant's office."

The board of lieutenants and sub-lieutenants costs them sixty francs a month, with at least five or six francs for wine and extras. Those who have no assistance from their families sometimes go without light and fire in their quarters, and walk about the gloomy streets, or yawn in the cafés, and look enviously at the names of more fortunate people in the directory.

The most lucky are the steady-going country folk, who re-enlist, and at forty-two, after serving three terms, with a pension and a bonus, go back to their homes, buy a bit of land, and marry.

FROM RENNES TO REDON.

THIS is a charming country. The Vilaine meanders through it, and there are little green hills alternating with green hollows, with a delightful absence of regularity, which is full of caprice and imagination. The cool running water has strange dark tints, and a sort of intermitting turbulence. The meadows, constantly freshened by mists and rain, are framed with hedges of oak. Rain, or the weeping of the mist, forever descends upon the green oak summits. Verdure succeeds to verdure, and in their uniformity of fresh life, half-smiling and half-sad, there is a pleasing casualness, a quaint diversity of outline, caused by the uneven soil and the patterns of the fields. These remnants of the primitive forest give one glimpses every now and then of the ancient region of the Mabinogion, and of the Breton poems. The still and limpid waters, in their cups of green grass, and under the shade of innumerable oaks, must have wakened strange visions in unsophisticated minds, like that of Merlin and Vivien. Who can understand all that a spring has to say to a poet in the forest wilds?

Near Redan the lande begins. The granite belltower, flanked with smaller turrets, stands out grey and gloomy, pointing upwards to the pale misty sky, laden with heavy clouds, which drag themselves over the tree-tops. Then the trees disappear, or are but few and stunted, a scattered handful of pines, dwarfed and dwindling oaks and undergrowth. Next, for hours at a time, the lande, covered with heath and furze. The prickly litter of the furze collects in ugly heaps; the heath spreads far and wide its rough carpet of violet and red. There is no soil; every here and there the dry rock comes to the surface, surging up and down as far as the eye can reach, with no life-sustaining layer of mould to cover it. Desolate and deserted hollows and heights follow each other in succession, under a gloomy veil of melting fog. When there is water it is impure; the unbroken rock beneath prevents it from escaping; and it spreads itself in stagnant marshes, in little threads of green across the yellow unwholesome vegetation, which clings to the rock like a sickly skin, in lumpy quagmires, alternately overflowing and dry.

A few lines of wretched trees follow the course of this useless oozing water. Now and then a melancholy range of hills is dotted with moss-grown, weather-beaten rocks. A whispering grove of firs looks bare, with its lanky stems and shadeless tree-tops. It is like the north of Scotland without mountains. A few wild cattle, as in Scotland, dot with white and red the monotonous gloom of the furze; a woman is running along with bare feet; and through a patch of buckwheat, where the land is capable of tillage, a labourer in wooden shoes and an enormous hat, both discoloured by constant rain, creeps along like a phantom in the mud. But, as in Scotland, here also, delightful clumps of rich violet heather smile amidst the dry bones of the obtrusive rock.

VANNES.

YESTERDAY I was at Carnac. But before I speak of it I will set down my impressions of Vannes.

The most striking female type is that of the religious sisters. They are pale of complexion, sometimes rather sallow and sickly, often extremely delicate. Some of the younger ones give one the idea of an ascetic Madonna, with a slender neck like that of Joan of Naples, long, thin, and altogether charming, with a remarkably sweet voice, modest downcast eyes, a quivering sensibility, amounting at times to painful shyness. The effect is delightful, and one feels that these are sensitive souls.

At Carnac, for instance, there was a girl with an ague, sitting silent and motionless at the kitchen window of the inn, with her head resting on her thin hand, dark circles round her eyes, yellow as new wax, like the nuns of Delaroche in his Cenci pictures. Her cousin, who waited on us at table, had a dainty chin, the most delicate lines, an exceedingly modest manner, and a voice of excellent pitch. Everything she said or did was calm and precise, and it was the same with the landlady. French is learnt in the schools as befits a literary tongue; the women speak it with delightful purity, with no provincial accent.

Physical placidity and the refinement of a mystic —these are the striking and by no means uncommon features.

In the young girls, and especially amongst the peasantry, the face is without a wrinkle, as pure as those of the mediæval Madonnas. They have the pale transparent complexion of a forest flower, sheltered and unceasingly lulled by shade. Most faces here are irregular, with large nose and small mouth; they are odd, and even ugly; but, when they smile, they light up as pleasantly as a cloudy sky penetrated by the sun. When humour, or even sometimes when malice passes over them, the fine effect is indescribable.

I saw a few handsome, strong, thorough types, with well-shaped heads, but these always showed the immobility of the primitive race. They look you full in the face, or else the fierce eyes are lowered; there are no sidelong, sheepish looks.

The dress of a sister is generally black, with long straight folds; they wear an apron reaching upwards to the throat, and fastened by pins at the shoulders;

a reddish or brown shawl, with the corners gathered into the bodice; a hood of white linen on the head, with flaps which cover the cheeks. At Vannes, it ends in long streamers, which float behind them. It is all very simple and tasteful—just cloth wound round the body and linen to cover the hair.

I attended mass at Vannes. The church was crowded. Near the entrance the men knelt on both knees, telling their beads and muttering their prayers, with sober look, quiet as the rigid body of a man in a trance. In the porch a poor, gouty, bent old man, in a sort of chair, with his long grey hair falling on his neck, mutters gravely with closed eyes, immersed in thought and counting his beads, whilst the other hand clasps his brazen crucifix.

An old woman, partly crippled, crouches against the stone wall, counts her beads, and mumbles a piece of bread. She looks like a witch.

A blind man had found his way to the front, and there, as close as he could come to the high altar, kneeling with straight back, mutters as he drinks in the holy atmosphere of the place.

Women, girls, and men file past the font, crossing themselves with the utmost reverence. Never a face is raised, except by the grand ladies of the town; not a look is allowed to wander; they walk past, cross themselves, and fall upon their knees with devout gravity and simplicity. Two or three pretty young girls, with their camellia tints blanched by the staring white of their hoods, with their fixed impassioned eyes, with their innermost soul breathing through its frail envelope, fill you with stupefaction and concern. The primitive virgin and the modern woman, the extremes of innocence and sensibility—what an appeal, and what a contrast! Side by side, the face, the attractions of a duchess in her boudoir, and the eyes of a child, or of a lamb.

The men wear black jackets and trousers, and an enormous black hat. The effect is funereal. Sometimes you see red lapels to the waistcoat, and the striped blue and brown breeches of the ancient Gaul. No necktie is worn; the big white neckband touches the hair and the ears. The hair often reaches the neck and shoulders in long locks, or in a single mop.

How the difference is impressed upon us! We went into a draper's shop. The girl who waited upon us is a native of Normandy, matter-of-fact and cheerful, but decidedly vulgar.

"There is no dancing here," she says; "the girls and women would think themselves lost if they were to dance. Not one of them would stay away from mass on Sunday; but they are light-fingered folk.

We have to keep our eyes open. They would not steal money, but anything in a shop is fair game."

According to an official whom I saw at Rennes, Brittany furnishes more recruits for the vice of the capital than any other part of France. In the country places brothers and sisters sleep in the same rooms, and the results may be imagined. At festivals, at the Pardons,[1] drunkenness is very common, and that leads to what is worse.

After further observation I should say that the typical distinction is due to the white complexion and transparency of the skin, to the delicacy of the chin, which ends in a point, and to the smallness of all the organs concerned in eating and drinking. The long and mobile mouth is very expressive, owing to the thinness of the lips; the eyes are of a dull or quiet blue.

At Vannes there are some traces of the ancient Breton town; it was mentioned to me as typical.

In the first place there are the old streets around the Church of Saint-Pierre. As at Auray, the houses have three or four low storeys. The upper ones over-

---

[1] There were 40,000 pilgrims at Notre-Dame d'Auray on July 28, who bivouacked in the open air.

hang the lower, so that there is not more than five feet between the gutters of the two roofs. There is not much light, and too little air.

These houses are of wood and clay, anything but substantial; there is often a storey which bends in and totters, or falls outward. Two houses separated by a narrow alley have sunk against each other, so that they have had to be stayed with beams. One comes upon narrow bulging steps, indescribable recesses and lairs, back-courts and lanes, the oddest jumble imaginable. These are relics of mediævalism, caprice, and contempt for health.

Against constant wind and rain, many houses are caparisoned with slates, wings, and extra roofs; the cracked and moss-grown slates rattle up and down, and the house looks like a half-scaled lizard. The oldest of those in the market-place have gabled fronts, so that one can appreciate their original elegance. The scaly head of these houses stands out stiff with its blue slates, above the yellow plaster and small-paned windows. You will see a statue of a saint surmounting a gable; a carved flower is conspicuous like a standard, or the projecting deity of the house. Such a building may be a strange and sickly being, and possibly spurious, but still it is alive.

Indeed, the Middle Age was an attic of the Muses.

Close to Saint-Pierre you turn aside from the street, and find the roof-gutters of the opposite houses touching each other.

There are other signs which show analogous feeling, though they are more recent in date. There is a Renaissance window springing from the roof of one house, which is rich in design, and, with its bars of sculptured stone, is no mere hole for the admission of light and air, but an existence, complete and interesting, on its own account. The flight of steps at the Town-hall has a double baluster, sinuous like that at Fontainebleau, and is furnished with finely-twisted, wrought-iron bars. A grand flight in the market-square, which once distinguished the front of a citizen's mansion, stands out across the pavement, which it usurps with its moss-grown flags, carrying tufts of grass in all the crevices.

We went down to the harbour, a long creek of the sea with a river flowing into it, and bordered by an avenue of elms extending over three-quarters of a mile. They are old, straight-grown, respectable elms, with as little character as the old town-houses running beside them. When the avenue ends the canal grows wider; there are two or three ships building close to the bank; the pale still water stretches out to the horizon between the two flat coasts. A ship has been left by the tide, resting against the muddy dock-side. Its black rigging is the only object which stands out clearly against the dying vapours of the murky sky, or against the broken background in which the dull greens of gorse, heather, and broom, with a few tree-tops here and there, lose themselves behind a shifting fog, now shrivelling as it yields its moisture to the clouds, now flickering like a phantom fire, lit by a fleeting sunbeam. There is a reek from the broad margin of silt, left bare by the ebbing tide, and the slimy bottom shines with inky lights. The dark standing water in the middle of the winding track slumbers with infected breath in the silent and deserted port.

FROM AURAY TO CARNAC.

AURAY is a pretty little town, built on two hillsides; between them flows a river, crossed by an old bridge. When the tide flows out the boats are left high and dry on the beach. There were constant showers; the old granite houses overhanging their foundations, the tumble-down cottages in the steep and winding lanes, the fresh green vegetation on the river banks, all bear witness to the never-ending wet.

We set out at nine in the morning, as the sunlight began to sift through the fog. The country greeted us like a poor but pretty girl, smiling through her tears, though we knew that the tears would break out afresh. A pleasant glow settles on the moist plain, and the purple heather, the yellow gorse and dandelions, the flowering broom, vary the old primitive green with mingled hues, deep and silky as those of a rich carpet. This rich vegetation, with its jumble of coloured designs on a dull background, is strangely pleasing to the sight; and it breathes out a vague odour almost imperceptibly sweet. The heavy crops of food-plants look coarse beside these delicate touches of wild nature.

There are scattered firs on the lande exposed to the sun; sleepy marshes dotted with green and white by the myriad shoots and snow-capped bushes. Fields of stubble, bare of all but a few blackening yellow stalks, alternate with patches enclosed by loose stone walls, or, still more frequently, by banks on which venerable bushes of furze grow close and thick, sometimes as high as a man, gnarled and bristling, crowding one upon another, covering up their old withered growth by many a new off-shoot, and trenching on the pasture-land by that incessant fleecing of their shaggy surface. I am never tired of looking at the rough massing of these hardy denizens of the soil, obstinate as the Breton granite, which stand guard over the property of man, themselves the imperishable children of the lande. Sometimes amidst their bristling ranks the summit of an oak rears itself on high, or a little pine, or a slender clump of shrubs. It is life, but poor and struggling life, covered with a monotonous grey tint. Only now and again, a young pine of softest green smiles at you from the gloomy border.

As we approach Carnac, every field bristles with

its stony barriers. The Celtic remains have been plundered to build these walls. It is calculated that two thousand menhirs have been destroyed, whilst eleven or twelve hundred remain. We examined the two longest rows. The longest of all stretches within sight of the sea. There are five rows of stones running east and west, set upright, with a good distance between them. Some have been overthrown. The largest are ten feet high, and all are rude, uncut stones, set in the soil on one end. The sight is not interesting on its own account; the blocks at Fontainebleau are vaster, and have a far grander effect. But, historically, these stones are very striking. It must have been a barbaric age that could be satisfied with such a temple. Is it the product of the age of stone, before men had discovered the metals? Or is it the work of Druids, who, accustomed to live in the woods without any covered temple, desired on this treeless plain to imitate the forest cloisters, and put on record their crude geometrical notions? In any case, these blocks were moved from place to place by the bare arms of savages, with the sole assistance of rollers. Here their fighting men were gathered together; here they had their human sacrifices; and the mist, the furze, the blue bay on the horizon, are the same for us as they were for them.

At the top of the hill a few houses are perched amongst the largest blocks, and these straight lines mark the boundaries of the gardens. One house has enclosed its acre within four of these gigantic stones; vegetables grow there, and fields of millet surround them, with their pale-hanging tufts, and fowls are roosting on them. It is a striking effect; this bit of ordinary culture and civilisation makes one realise how far we are removed from that barbaric age. It would be impossible to picture a monument more closely akin to Nature; if it were not for the regularity and the orientation of these lines, the temple might be a moraine. And was a Greek *temenos*, a primitive *templum* of the Etruscan or Roman, very different in character?

On the hillside, a little further inland, are a few great dolmens—circles of rude stones set up on end, with an enormous flat stone, equally rude, resting upon them like a sort of lid, but touching them only at three or four points. Anything more primitive could scarcely be imagined; there are similar arrangements produced by Nature, where she has piled her rocks at hazard.

There is an entrance into a lower cavity, here and there not unlike a drain. Papuans or Fijians might select such a spot for their sacrifices. Were these places tombs? In a neighbouring house we were shown a gold necklace, a Gallic "torques," which had been found here. Perchance in these depths they slaughtered prisoners and slaves over the body of their master!

The arms which moved these masses of stone must have been brawny and vigorous. Some of these dolmens are on the summit of the hill, within sight of the sea. Was there some pious hope of resurrection expressed in this approximation to the setting sun and the infinite ocean? The Druids believed in the immortality of the soul, and its re-incarnation. The question whether these monuments are really Gallic is worthy of study. They may even date from the Jade Period, the first appearance of the Gauls in the west. We are tempted to abolish the intervening culture by a stroke of the pen, and to fix our thoughts on the time when the human species wandered in the woods, not far removed from the vanished aurochs and moose-deer.

We went down into the Quiberon peninsula, and spent the afternoon on the beach. For a league and a half our carriage jolted over the lumpy plain, rough with grass and bushes, and out of sight of the sea. There was not a tree to be seen; the broom and furze are barely a foot above the ground. Trenches have been made to induce the growth of small trees in the hollows, but nothing came of it.

At rare intervals, in some sheltered spot, we caught sight of a diminutive fir, which had attained a height of eighteen inches. The everlasting winds destroy or stunt every scrap of vegetation. It is all as desolate as a steppe.

Presently we reach an isthmus, with the sea on either side of us. The eastern sea is without a ripple, intensely blue, the richest and deepest blue imaginable. The western sea foams and dashes incessantly against the shore, and the Bretons call it the Mer Sauvage. It is one bright and flashing green, as far as the eye can reach, and is broken by dark rugged islands. As it nears the coast it rises above the seaweeds in violet waves of splendidly varying tints, fringed with silver above, and breaking in a shower of sunlight. The whole coast is wreathed in a coronal of lurid violet and silvery bronze. A million grains of salt sparkle in the white sand of the sea-shore. White-footed women are gathering the dry seaweed with their rakes; the briny wind sweeps in their faces, with a mist of foam and a resonant harmonious murmur.

On the other side of the isthmus the sea is as level in parts as a mirror of sapphire, whilst in other parts it is streaked with almost imperceptible quiverings, which cross each other. A tiny wave flows over the polished sand, then retreats with a gentle whisper. The water is so transparent that one can see the shells beneath it, the burrowing crabs, and the little points of granite which break the surface. The flowering grass tufts the crevices of rock, and overhang the azure sea. A boat sways upon the water; a few smacks hover on the horizon. But the finest detail of the picture is the deep strong blue which cuts so clean, and with so bold a contrast, into the dull green of the lande, and the pale greys of the coast-line. It is the only surface that reflects the light; everything else extinguishes it. The coast, with its rays of white walls, and seamed with rocks, is like some rough basin or chalky hollow which, by queer mischance, contains a precious liquor.

A strange contrast is afforded when we leave Britanny and approach Savenay, across the flat and fertile plain of the Loire. It is moist and verdant meadow-land, dotted with flocks, and watered by the broad and peaceful stream. Near Nantes the houses have an air of wealth and comfort; lines of ships are at anchor in the Loire, and we are soon amongst the quays, the shops, the stacks of coal, the crowded and promiscuous trade. Then our train runs slowly through the middle of the town, separated from the quayside and the people by a low barrier. After that, the Sunday crowd, the close-built, six-storeyed houses with scores of windows, the smoky chimneys, the toil and contrivances of a population of a hundred thousand.

THE CATHEDRAL OF NANTES.

THERE is a tomb of Francis the Second (died in 1488), Duke of Britanny, and of his wife, by Michel Colomb. The duke and duchess, in their ducal robes and coronets, lie peacefully sleeping, with their hands clasped.

It is a commonplace carving, but full of life and sincerity, with a smack of Italy in the general idea, and in the fine simplicity of detail. The figures are evidently portraits; the calm of eternal sleep is fully realised. Throughout the fifteenth century there was a most vivid sentiment of moral realism. But the pointed nose, the sharply peaked chin, the too prominent eyes, the lack of amplitude and resolution in the features—all this is what we have been taught to expect in the mediæval burgess. The four female forms at the corners are life size, and have heads of the same pattern: the antique type was not known to these sculptors. They just copied the forms that pleased them amongst their neighbours, and so attained to a thing sufficiently admirable in itself, which had both originality and individuality. It is easy to believe in the existence of these people, and in their souls. Almost all the female figures have just the measure of limited feminine intellect which is usual in France, with the familiar little cushion of flesh beneath the chin, the pointed nose, the supple hands, with too much of bone and sinew. It is the modern type, and perhaps the true art of sculpture was to work upon it. Excellent, too, in all this art is the profound study of draperies, the rich original conception and thoughtful arrangement of every kind of costume, antique or feudal or provincial. It is the same in Italy and Germany, in the etchings of Pollajuolo, Mantegna, and Albert Dürer. There is broad and deep feeling in the sixteen dark figures of crouching monks, repellent, with an expression full of suffering, weighed down by their robes, crushed by many prayers and the terrors of religion—wrecks of humanity smothered by the frock, and shrivelled by dread of the divine vengeance!

FROM NANTES TO ANGERS.

I HAD the carriage all to myself, and enjoyed three hours of greater pleasure than I have known for a long time.

Emerging from Britanny, with the memory full of those over-saturated landscapes, lean lands flooded with stagnant water, a thin soil on a bed of old rock, a drowned verdure dotted with poor crops of wheat, mud hovels, wretched cabins, pale and sickly forms of fanatics or idiots, drunken bodies and inflated heads, rude survivals from the sixteenth century, we enter a land of abundance and settled joy.

Lazy Loire keeps us company on the right, a broad blue river, as level as a sheet of glass, covered with large square-sailed boats, sailing slowly against the stream. There are round green masses on every hand, osier-beds, birch-trees, little groves, with white castles on the hills, rose-trees and clumps of ornamental trees on the slopes, verdant isles and banks of sand, wayward water quivering in the light, which throws its blue arms about the green. The river goes softly, in almost motionless broad reaches, and the spirit glides along in harmony with it. The air is warm: vaguely we remember our gondola in Venice, with the music, and the ladies in brocaded silk, and the pearls that almost hid their arms. Thus floated the Valois between castle and castle, in their gorgeous barges.

As the shadows lengthen, earth and sky put on deeper tints of brown and purple. The darkened trees cast their gloomy image on the unruffled stream. An imperceptible mist breathes over the dull gold and suffused pink above the vanished sun. The moon unveils herself in a white fleece of clouds, and scatters the first drops of a shower of light. All around us the willows hang their veil of dark velvet. There is no colour left beyond the dim reds and russets, sinking into the pale blue tint that lies cold and calm on the horizon.

THE PICTURE-GALLERY AT ANGERS.

HERE I admired most of all the minor French artists of the eighteenth century:—Lancret, Chardin, Greuze, and Watteau. They are all charming, distinguished, refined, with a light, deft touch, somewhat dim in colour, yet harmonious. It is the efflorescence of the age of gallantry.

In Lancret, note especially the ease and grace with which, amidst the general dulness of his colouring, the tones vary incessantly and imperceptibly, like a sun-touched mist slowly evaporating. There is no striving for effect, but only an unlimited caprice. A little patch of red, and two black points, create a face. The sketch tells everything and tells it so quickly! The foliage is but a pale green or yellow-green detail, a vague subordinated shape. One feels that the painter has no plan, merely advancing by little touches to produce a general effect, a harmony of twinkling drapery, the spirit and grace of the central figures.

Watteau, is a better colourist by far, or at any rate he has reached a greater height. His hues are more intense. Like the others, only more distinctly, he is a Fleming.

There are some casts of the works of David of Angers.

They bore me. You have here the historic or emphatic school which preceded 1848, which was false, or at least inadequate.

Yet a day might be spent in studying his bronze medallions; there are four or five hundred of them.

All the remarkable men or women of his time are here in profile, liberally interpreted. They give us the history of the age, an age of excitement and hard work. They reveal the inner workings and endless diversity of the soul.

Other large terra-cotta busts are very noteworthy. There is Armand Carrel, for instance, lank, with high cheek-bones, full-faced, pointed and keen as a blade, sharp and bitter; and the heroic bust of David the elder, wearing a moustache, hollow-eyed, with deep sockets and bloated cheeks, an eager Republican giant, full of spirit and action, bold and explosive.

TOULOUSE.

THERE is too much to say. I have seen the Picture Gallery and the Exhibition at Toulouse, have dined with new-made friends, driven into the country, and so on.

I may say at once that the Toulouse Gallery contains a few fine pictures which I had not previously seen:—a Carrache, a portrait by Mirevelt, a curious portrait of Descartes as a young man, and a fine Van der Meulen. There are a few Italian canvases. One of them is a charming little Guardi, in the room above. It is a Venetian holiday, a sort of regatta of gondolas, around a vast gilded Bucentaur, like a sea-monster, encased in scales of gold. On board are signors and councillors in their robes, and a number of masked figures, male and female, black masks and pale silk robes, with little masculine hats on their heads. Round about them sport the steel-prowed gondolas. The sea glows with softened brightness, beneath a sky of tender blue, spread with tranquil fleecy clouds. And like a precious frame to the picture, or like a capriciously-woven border of lace, Venice surrounds the broad sea canvas with St Mark, the palaces of the Procurators, the quays and domes, the laughing throng on the broad pavement.

There are two excellent portraits by Gros, of himself and his wife. He has long curls, a soft black hat, reminding one, by its extravagance, of Van Dyck and the Flemish School, and a broad soft muslin band twisted round his neck. He is pale of complexion, with fine eyes, ardent, and full of genius. She wears a straight red Empire dress, and is round and fresh; just a little snappish, despotic, and narrow-minded, as French women are apt to be, but all toned down by the wealth and bloom of youth. You may call her his mistress if you will, but she is a mistress dignified by a painter and a lover. The whole picture is simple and substantial. Contrast it with the Courbets and Ricards in the Toulouse Exhibition, pictures of our own contemporary style, which aim at the petty or the strange. It is the same kind of contrast that you get between the styles of Balzac and Michelet.

The two pictures of Couture and Eugène Delacroix gave me but little pleasure. They are evidently tentative or improvised. The painters do not know enough.

My new friends took me to the Exhibition in order to see the hall. It is in the old Jacobin Convent, which has been re-decorated this year. It was formerly the cavalry barracks. It is a vast red-brick building, with big red buttresses, almost windowless; for most of the old windows have been built up. It dates from 1238, and was built for the Dominican Inquisition. They gave me several pamphlets, with the story of a sick woman who was burnt alive—admirable!

The church is a masterpiece, very original in style. It is divided into two naves by a row of very high round columns, like the trunks of palm-trees, spreading out into fillets above. On this slender support the whole dome rests. The last column ends in a cluster of twenty-three arches, supporting the apse. So high are they, and so straight, so white with their crown of black arches against the white walls, that these columns are like an enormous firework, or the continuous play of a fountain. Nothing finer can be imagined than their curves, nothing richer than their clusters. When they have removed the floor which cuts off a storey from its height, we shall have perhaps the finest Gothic nave in France—especially if the windows are opened again, and filled with painted glass. The columns are so slender that the two naves are virtually one. The large windows, the mingled hues of gold and purple from the panes, will fill this void with a sort of glory. It will glow like a

TOULOUSE.

UNIV. OF
CALIFORNIA

tabernacle, as the Sainte-Chapelle of St Louis glows to-day, so richly adorned, so radiant, so like a shrine overflowing with radiance from the Virgin, and the angels, and the Deity. This epoch of the Middle Age was perhaps the most triumphant and ecstatic. It was the zenith of the power of the Church. Here, no doubt, Gothic art was combined with some reminiscence from Rome, or some half-defined Arab innovation. It is worth considering whether in these high expanding trunks and these clustered fillets there is not some distant imitation of the sculptured palms of the Alhambra.

Two little rose-windows in the front of the building are intact, or restored in keeping with the fragments which have survived. That on the left, purple and ochre in its hues, is of matchless magnificence. The deep yellow, tinged with red, and lighted from without, is as fine, in its contrast with the massive darkness of the vast wall through which it breaks, as a flaming southern horizon reflected in a lake under the setting sun.

There is a delightful cloistered promenade, not very lofty, supported by a row of slender columns in couples, and surmounted by a roof of old red tiles. This red tone of the tiles, and of the old bricks which have long been exposed to the sun, is universal at Toulouse. Now the venerable walls are scaling; the

Q

surface is broken by the falling out of bricks; and the bright colour of those which remain is set off by the darkness of the gaps. Ivy clambers up them in broad shining mantles; a cypress rears its pyramid hard by, and young green leaves cling gaily to the dark old crumbling wall.

This is a city and a race well endowed for the culture of art. There is a Conservatoire of Music, which sends promising recruits to Paris and to Italy. Toulouse has a school of painting and drawing, a large number of artists, a good gallery, and many fine monuments. The girls will sing the airs of five or six operas after hearing them on the stage; and there are plenty of amateurs with musical taste, who can play an opera on the piano more or less correctly.

I have just seen Carcassonne and Cette. The bright sunshine, the mountains, the sea, the soft horizons, the vivacious inhabitants, with their gossiping off-hand ways, their ringing musical talk, and many other features, bespeak a race which is partly Italian, though of lighter build. Their union with Frenchmen of the north prevents them from being more strongly southern in type; it cut them adrift in the thirteenth century, and they have never been able to recover themselves. Their aristocracy live inert and old-fashioned in the country, and, having little money, they have grown miserly: they do not buy pictures or support the musical festivals. If they could have developed their mediæval constitution, and lived split up into little independent sovereignties, stimulated by the municipal sentiment, retaining their local speech, and creating their own literature and manners, we should have one nation the more, another standard of feeling, another art. It is part of the price which we have had to pay for centralisation in France. These people live in the grooves and under the regulations devised for the north.

In respect of religion also they are Italian. I believe there are sixty-four convents in Toulouse. In the country I saw the monastery of the Trappists, who never leave its precincts, but till the land, confess through a little grating of their cell, rise at one in the morning, and make up their sleep with an hour or two in the afternoon. I saw a woman wandering in the garden, in her long robe of yellowish white, like a poor spectre, bowed and sickly, amidst the bright and happy landscape. There are four-score of them. What a gap this makes in family life! A young lady told us of three of her friends who had taken the veil. They are received at the age when women are wont to break out into eccentricity, and when their heads are full of enthusiasm. One of them said to her mother, who was weeping over her:

"Dear mamma, you would have given me to a husband, but I would rather have Jesus Christ for my husband. We shall all be together again in Heaven."

At the age of vague desires, Jesus, divine and yet human, is the incorporeal husband to whom the veiled cravings of modesty aspire.

There is a preacher here who has a great reputation. My friends compare him to George Sand's Father Onofrio in "Mademoiselle de la Quintinie." He makes his converts with a certain amount of force, and is sometimes subjected to forcible reprisals by fathers or husbands. Not long since, after he had ended his sermon, he led off his audience to the cemetery, and there, with the tombs lighted up by torches, he spoke of the worms, the rotting body, and the flames of hell. One lady, who had recently lost her eldest son, was carried away in a fit of hysterics. At Cahors, one of the handsomest girls in the town resolved to take the veil. When she came to the church for that purpose, dressed in white bridal robes, the men began to murmur in pity—

"It is nothing but a murder!"

So great was the disturbance that the ceremony could not be completed.

It is the gay world, and especially balls, to which the clergy mainly object. There was a young girl of fifteen who had become very religious; she used to attend her catechism class with great regularity, and the priest urged her not to go to a ball. Her parents gave a dance, and she wept because she was expected to take part in the festivities. Her confessor backed her up; but the father insisted that she should go, because her mother wished it. But he promised that his daughter should only dance twice. On the following day her imagination had resumed its empire; she was saluted in the streets by her partners of the previous night, and she was no longer an ardent catechumen.

There are a surprising number of street preachers in Toulouse; we are in the midst of a retreat. I can count a score of them as I stand in the square of the Capitol; and there are others in the streets around.

One of the most important convents is that of Marie-Réparatrice. A sister must have fifty or sixty thousand francs before she can enter it. They succeed each other constantly in the chapel, in order to worship and sing hymns. They may be seen through the railings, and it is a poetic and attractive spectacle. They wear silk shoes, and elegant robes of blue and white. The essence of Catholicism in the south is to catch men by displays of pomp, by the delight of the eyes, by a timely diversion of the sex instinct, and by the fear of hell when the flesh is growing weak. Money comes to the clergy in great measure from old men who are beginning to think about death.

CARCASSONNE.

THIS old town, a strong hill-fortress of the Middle Age, is almost deserted. There are some eighteen hundred poor creatures, weavers for the most part, in old houses of lath and plaster. Rudely-built cottages, tottering or supported by props, damp and unclean, cling to the old walls; and in the narrow street, amidst filth and unwholesome refuse, dirty ragged children wander about, attended by swarms of flies, under a leaden sun, which bakes and browns all this human clay. It is a fourteenth-century Ghetto.

On a steep, red, bare, abandoned hill, the city stands within its double circuit of feudal walls, a formidable rampart, encrusted with towers, bristling with parapets and battlements, all blackened in the sun. You have to climb up a slope, roughly strewn with sharp pebbles, which must have been impossible in the Middle Age for all but mounted men-at-arms, or waggons drawn by oxen. Narrow posterns are enclosed between great towers, and the portals are strongly built, with pointed arches. Only here and there one comes upon a few fine curves of a floriated mullion, or an arched window with delicate little columns. The general effect is rude, forbidding, and sombre.

The good folk lived here as in an eagle's nest, happy enough so long as they were not slain: that was the luxury of the feudal age. The towers have two or three storeys. Each tower and each floor of a tower could be separately defended; every enclosure could stand a siege. There are embrasures for the crossbow-men, sloping battlements for the launching of stones, little tunnels through which to pour the molten lead or boiling oil, trap-stairs without egress, so as to snare the foe into a sort of pit, in which they could be shot down with arrows, round towers for a sudden rally, or for the bodyguard of the count or captain, notches in the stone wall for the wooden shields which covered the archers. The massing of stonework, the manifold devices of attack and defence, are amazing. All this was very necessary against a Cœur de Lion or a Du Guesclin, who, clad in mail, covered by his shield, would press forward in spite of arrows, and hew down the doors with his battle-axe. Dimly across the interval one can imagine the assaults, the dense body of troops, the clang of iron beneath the posterns, within the storeyed towers, along these winding stairs, and the combats of well-nigh invulnerable men, who smote each other like Cyclops at their forge.

On the ground floor of one of those towers you may still behold a massive iron chain, fixed into a pillar, the ring of which has been vainly bitten by axe and file. They found a skeleton here, below the chain. It was once a prison of the Inquisition.

Unfortunately the circuit of walls is being restored. The new clean stonework, so out of place to-day, looks like a piece of stage scenery. But the other parts, still intact, burnt by the sun, tanned and reddened by time, incrusted with yellow lichen, eaten into by wind and rain, proudly vaunt their broken outline, their capricious dilapidation, their crumbling quaintness, their rough walls. The light that clings to the prominent points and smoother masses flashes out from the black crevices; withered plants droop from the disjointed parapets; a square perpendicular tower stands out stiff into the blue from amidst the dismantled blocks. Nature has resumed possession of this building of man's, has given it harmony, poured out upon it her caprice, her confusion, her careless touches, her infinite variety of form, her abundant wealth of hue.

St Nazaire is an attractive church. Its nave, with

arches scarcely pointed, is either Roman or the next thing to it. The choir is later, and has grand windows filled with old painted glass. The idea was ever the same, to make the choir a picture of Paradise, full of bright light and celestial glory. In one window are Adam and Eve, in their primeval condition, very obese and very placid. Half-way up the pillars of the choir there are statues, simple and decently good, with a fair amount of expression, and well proportioned, bearing manifest testimony to the fourteenth century and the completion of the building.

In the sacristy is a monument to a bishop whose body has been exhumed. The stone figure is simple and realistic. Underneath is a somewhat crude procession of little stone figures, approaching the deathbed, diminutive forms in relief, much in the manner of the successors of Giotto, artists in their infancy. There was a crypt containing tombs, a sort of waterway, with a roof supported by short columns.

The whole of the outside is being restored; and above the outer transept they have patched up a series of very grotesque and ugly heads—a mediæval comedy. But on the right hand there is a sort of built-up window, ending in an acute angle, with flower-work of the most original and attractive kind. The effect is Gothic, compromised by Latin traditions. There is the same thing at Béziers. On every side we have traces of an Italy which did not reach her full development.)

For compensation, there are new buildings, grand gardens, splendid avenues of great plane-trees with scaling bark, watercourses to keep them constantly fresh, a murmuring busy crowd, cafés, plenty of carriages and diligences packed with gentlemen of a sort and respectable peasants, and any amount of cheerful gossip and chaff. It is all very poor form, this latter-day town of the translated south, converted by the north to peace, civilisation, and prosperity.

And now Italy herself is yearning for this kind of thing!

CETTE.

AT eight in the evening I rowed alone on the lake of Thau, outside the town. It is a stretch of water bequeathed by the sea, three miles long by one mile in breadth. Clouds covered the whole sky; from time to time the moon peeped through a rent, fording from cleft to cleft, vanishing as soon as she appeared, after shedding a momentary stream of silver on the dark surface of the water. I could just make out the vast round dome of Heaven. The horizon of the land is but a narrow coal-black marsh. The heaving water and the dripping mist, and, overhead, the vast opaque masses of leaden cloud, fill up the round of space.

No words can describe the hue of the water on such a night as this—black, brown, but indistinct and rippling vaguely, easier to hear than to see. You can distinguish nothing from that vast wilderness of floating forms. Gradually the eyes become accustomed to the darkness, and catch the imperishable light which is always distilling from water. Like a glass in a closed dark chamber, like one of those sombre magic mirrors of unfathomable depth, it glows obscurely and mysteriously, but still it glows. The head of a tiny ripple, the back of a broad wave, the polished wall of a tranquil depth, the doubtful quiver of a pool, win some flash of brightness, reflect some far-off ray of undulating light; and all these feeble glimmers overlap and cross and melt into each other, and so, from the great wandering blackness, there emerges a sort of luminous pallor, as of a metal distinguished in the dark—an atom of imperceptible light, drowned in the heavy folds of the cloud, and in the commingling of far-away forms.

Twice or thrice the moon came forth, and her broad quivering beam was as that of a solitary lamp, lit up amongst black hanging draperies, in some prodigious dome of a mortuary chapel. On the horizon, like a procession of coffins and torches, halting at an immense distance, is the low, black, sleeping coast, with two or three lights at each corner of the catafalque.

There was a wonderful stillness on the broad canal by which I returned. Not a single boat, not a breath of wind was stirring. The lights of Cette were drawn out into long tremulous lines on the sheet of motionless water. The stillness of the dark and glowing stream touched me to the quick with mingled horror and pleasure. As I drew nearer to the town, and the black line of houses cut a bolder pattern out of the sky, the glitter and placidity of the water became yet more striking; and presently the canal was a trail of soft white light between two banks of gloomy shapes. What a contrast to my arrival on the previous day —sunset on the polished mirror of the lake, the fire of yellow and indigo on the horizon, reflected with more metallic and intense brightness on the resplendent surface, earth and sky lit up in every corner, and above this fluent splendour a pale, pacific, spotless azure, in which already sparkled the first javelin-points of the approaching host of stars.

A VISIT TO AIGUES-MORTES.

WE set out at six in the morning, and had a carriage drive of an hour and a half across the wide plain between Lunel and Aigues-Mortes. This plain is an old river deposit, embanked in the sixteenth century. In some places there is a depth of five metres of fertile soil. It is all laid down in vines. The stocks are as thick as your fist, and one branch will often yield ten litres of wine. In spite of the large quantity exported, it is so cheap that a hundred litres sold last year for five francs. There are not many poor people. The land is much subdivided, and recent extensions of trade have made everybody prosperous.

The landscape is not out of the common, or worthy of much remark. A great level tract, dotted here and there by a group of parasol-pines and white poplars; an occasional cypress, a row of plane-trees, a village surrounded by old broad walks, and set with beautiful trees. There are vines on every hand, self-supported, then fields of lucerne, and marshy lands, grazed by the horses of the Camargue. There is a round tower in the far horizon. On the right, a broken zigzag, showing the line of the distant mountains. But the effect is charming. There was a slight continuous breeze, which cooled and refreshed us. The quiet soft landscapes passed us like the visions of a dream; every shade of colour was fine and delicate, for the clear sky subdued the earthly tints. The roads stretch out before us in long white even bands; the silvered trunks of the plane-trees are tinted with a feeble green; the innumerable tamarisks, which fringe the roads and fields, are hempen-grey; the leaves of plane and poplar, as they turn in the breeze, display the dull white cotton of their under-sides. Little patches of flowers diversify the green fields with stripes of subdued amaranth. The long-stalked scented herbs make a soft blue border under the roadside hedges. The very houses, some white and new, others old and grey with time, the dull red roofs, the ash-grey farm-buildings, add their sombre tints to the softer harmonies of nature. Only the omnipresent light plays over the face of all things, and knows neither contrast nor limits. And the crowning sky is a pale and silky azure, rising imperceptibly into a bright unmixed blue, though its dome is streaked with slender veins, fine cloudlets drawn out like diaphanous gauze, as it were a delicate cocoon on the point of floating away.

The city walls are very curious, being almost as perfect as when they were built. The whole city is enclosed by them, as a protection against the floods; and from the top of the Constance Tower this multitude of low-lying roofs in their stone enclosure are like so many draughts on a draught-board.

The fortifications remind one of those of Carcassonne, which dates, like this town, from the time of Saint Louis. There is a long, loopholed, battlemented wall, flanked at intervals by round towers. Each gate has its tower; the original form is preserved in all the arches; and at one corner of the city there is another vast round tower of two storeys, with a flat roof and a watch-tower. This is the ancient citadel, in which a defence could be maintained even if the city were taken. Nothing could be more simple or sensible than the plan of its construction. It is just an enormous wall pierced by loopholes, and thick enough to contain a flight of steps. At each stage there is a lofty stone hall, the pointed roof springing from the sides in a cluster of arches. There is a dungeon in the centre, and a vast fireplace and chimney. A dim light falls from above, and through a row of short arched bays

R

looking upon the steps. This round hollow shell of bare stone, this cold grey light which seems to slumber for ever unchanged, is decidedly forbidding. Amidst the prevailing obscurity, the frowning stone and the stern outlines of the tower, it is a strange relief to come upon a boss of carved flowers, supporting the arches where they spring from the wall.

From the platform above there is a view of the plain, bounded on one horizon by a scarcely perceptible violet line of mountains. On the other sides, far as the eye can reach, save where it sinks into the boundless sea, the green plain is parcelled out by watercourses, which glitter like sheets of polished silver; and the ocean spreads a broad mirror of sombre blue.

FROM ARLES TO MARSEILLES.

IN the museum at Arles are the ruins discovered in the theatre at Alyscamps, the ancient Gallo-Roman cemetery. The chief fragment is a head of Venus, very beautiful. The admirable fulness of the upper part of the cranium impresses one with a sense of the force and genius of the race which produced it. The mouth is small and half-open; the upper lip is rather full and prominent—it is almost the mouth of a tragic mask. The expressionless eyes, rounded cheeks, broad strong chin, are at once serious and simple in character. It is a woman of five-and-twenty, in the very bloom of youth. There is the idea of gravity, even of sadness, which belongs to animalism at rest.

The tomb of Apollo is fine. Above it stand the Nine Muses, much mutilated, but slender, tall as the women of the Primaticcio, their close drapery responding to the most sensitive and graceful motions of the supple body, of the balanced limb and bended knee. Oh the delicacy of the sculptor's art! How it wakens all that is natural and vivid, all the happiness and simplicity of life!

By contrast, the Christian tombs of the third and fourth centuries are singularly instructive. Is it possible that two centuries should have exhibited such a decay! Heads too big, feet clumsily set and out of proportion, stiff bodies, awkward limbs, silly expressions! There is no art here.

Saint-Trophime—The gabled façade, in Italian style, recalls Siena and Pisa, with the impression of elegance and solidity which is characteristic of that architecture. The portico, though its carvings are crude enough, is a masterpiece. We have an ancient ornate pediment, supported by heads of lions and goats. Above the door is a Christ, thin, conventional in the ecclesiastical sense, with bony knees and long thin feet, seated between two angels, who hold the Gospel before Him, and surrounded by quaint symbolic animals. The whole vault above His head is occupied by a double row of busts and winged heads of angels, with richly carved arabesque, whilst on either side are long descending series of saints, in attitudes of stiff monastic ecstasy. Nothing could be richer or more satisfying to the eye than this effect of figures and foliage. This multitudinous character is one of the best marks of the mediæval genius.

On the two sides are details which reminded me of a pulpit in San Nicolas at Pisa. On the right, the naked souls of the damned are fleeing from the presence of the Deity, fettered to a long iron chain, and driven by a repulsive, jeering demon. Opposite to these is a procession of sainted men and women in long robes, after the ancient manner—as in the pictures of the Campo Santo, or of Simon Memmius. There are several antique heads and accessories. Some of the figures are clad like Dacian kings of the third century; a few of the saints wear togas and folding robes. But almost all, unfortunately, have the grimace which was at this time becoming a convention of the art of sculpture. A strange blending of the Gothic and the antique is manifest throughout.

The exterior cannot be seen, for it is elbowed close by houses. But from the neighbouring cloister of Saint-Trophime you may distinguish a high square belfry of four storeys. This solid massive construction varies the whole impression; you realise, then, that you are in a southern land.

The cloister itself is one of the strangest of sights. It is a promenade about a square plot of grass, manifestly counting its age by centuries. The heavy stone wall and arched roof, supported by couples of slender columns, is clumsy enough. The architect had no feeling for harmonies and proportions; he simply groped amongst his instinctive tendencies and his conventional reminiscences. But the carving is especially barbarous. Several of the heads measure one-third, or even one-half of the trunk. In the Ascension of Christ they are pitiable and grotesque, giving one the idea of a caricature. In the Massacre of the Innocents, the executioners in their coats of mail look like shaggy beasts, with sheeps' heads. The gawky mothers, the jumble and confusion of the bodies, the riot of ignorance and caprice, the three horses of the Magi clapped one upon the other, the facial expressions reminding you of bewildered frogs, are things to be seen rather than described. Yet, even in such a medley and excess, you may appreciate the fervour which at that period revelled amongst the legends of the saints. There are a few fine figures at the angles of a pillar, and in particular a saint at the corner of a cistern, a dried skeleton with narrow sloping shoulders, with very little in the way of cheeks or chin, with barely any forehead, the eyes alone occupying most of the face, like a shrunken fakir consumed by his ecstasy, with lank marrowless bones, such as you see in an Indian ascetic. Amongst the smaller figures near to this is a poor corpse-like Christ, with great big eyes in an attenuated face, and St John leaning on

His bosom. On such ideas the faithful few were wont to feed their hearts. This belongs to the eleventh century, when the Normans and Hungarians carried all before them.

Arles is just like an Italian city. Irregular streets, tumbledown buildings, here and there the ruins of an arcade; in the public square two Roman columns, half buried in the wall; an old, dilapidated, weather-beaten city wall; an ancient square mediæval tower; hard by a theatre in ruins; a medley of houses on the rising ground; bare walls with scarcely a single window; a chaos of many centuries; a solitary fig-tree, and grass growing thick in the crevices.

I sat in the theatre, on the semicircle of the broad stone tiers. In front is all that remains of the stage—two columns of speckled marble supporting a fragment of entablature; by their side fragments of the shafts of the next two columns; beside these, the pediments of another row of columns which have disappeared; on the ground, fragments of fluted shafts. These relics suffice to show the general plan.

What a gap there is between this dramatic art and our own! Imagine 16,000 spectators here in the daylight; actors with masks and a sort of speaking-tube; a drama sung like a recitative at the opera;

bright flowing robes; groups of sculpture such as one can imagine from the Aldobrandini nuptial fresco, which Poussin copied. We ought to realise these material accessories of an ancient drama before venturing to say a word about it.

A theatre on the scale here indicated must have been more like a circus than any theatre of our day.

One impression dwells constantly in the eyes in all these towns and villages of the south—a greyness on a background of white, a grey effect even in the brilliant light. Cette is especially notable for this. In a white dusty street, with a keen brightness in the air, amidst the sudden flashes of light which, at certain angles, are like direct sunbeams, and beneath the predominant azure which vaults the sky, the houses have the appearance of plastered mud baked hard by the sun. Nothing could be more dull to look at than those grey walls, caked with ancient dust, relieved by very few windows, and surmounted by dim-coloured tiles.

At Arles, as at Avignon, all is Italian: it is France and not France. The steep rough streets, only half-lighted in the evening by distant flickering lamps, are like those of Rome and Perugia long dark passages, forbidding, full of twists and turns, as it were sewers of uncanny blackness. Water collects in the middle, and, as you advance through the dark, it is reflected from the uneven stones in lurid gleams. You are constantly coming upon forlorn nooks and corners. Other lanes are full of humming sounds, as of bees about to swarm. There are men and women at the mouths of their lairs, like so many shades, who fill the air with harsh resounding noise. As you pass there is an indistinct group of heads, a weird hovel with a few sticks of furniture quaking in the feeble yellow flicker of a lamp, a rickety staircase leading up into the blackness of darkness. And all day long the squares and streets are full of idle gossipers and loungers.

Yet at Marseilles, as at Cette, you have the delightful sparkling blue sea, which is the most beautiful thing in the world. I drove out between two examinations, and took a cup of coffee in the balcony of the Réserve. The sea was like a sheet of metal straight from the forge, all inlaid and damascened with shining arabesques. A million lights flashed over this embossed surface of deepest blue, as they flash over a richly chased cuirass. The tone varies from a dim clouded amethyst to a pure sapphire, thence to the green glitter of a turquoise, and to the soft pale silk which dies into the whiteness of the sky. And who shall find a comparison for that sky? When a lovely girl, in the freshness of her bloom, dressed in her bridal robes, has fixed her golden comb in her hair, strings of pearls round her throat, and diamonds in her ears, and when all her jewels flash upon her rosy pulsing flesh, she covers herself with a long white floating veil. But her face has filled the veil with light, and the gauze which is intended to conceal it does but lend it a new glory. So is it with these rocks and walls of marble under the misty air, which seizes the splendour of the sun, and pours it forth upon them.

The whole land has been consumed. Nothing but stones, rocky fragments, long denuded spines, which break through their tatters of dwindling growth. Plant-life has half disappeared, leaving but the carcass of the ground.

Civilisation is too ancient here; humanity has gnawed it to the bone. Yet at Marseilles it borrows new life, and the flesh is returning to it. The Crau is being fertilised, and devoted to vines, which yield a strong and spirituous wine. The dry plains are irrigated, and the Durance is brought into the town by an enormous aqueduct. Marseilles, like a mighty sucker, draws in new life and disperses it again. It has 260,000 inhabitants, and increases at the rate of 20,000 a year. Through the growth of Italy and Spain, the opening of the Isthmus of Suez, the revival of all the wasted and outworn countries of the Mediterranean, it will soon be a city of half-a-million. There is enormous activity and enterprise; they work on a grander scale than in Paris.

One evening at ten o'clock, under a bright moon and a cloudless sky, I followed the new street between the two harbours. A hill was levelled in making it. The city sold the sites for twenty million francs. The Pereira Brothers are spending thirty or forty millions in building houses, all of them simultaneously, each enormous, in six storeys, and, reckoning by my own hotel, with staircases of a hundred and fifty steps. They are constructed of large hewn stone, white and carved. Some are finished, others half finished, others again just rising from their foundations, amidst scaffolding, cranes, steam-winches, supplies of flowing water. The street is like some Baalbec incomplete and deserted. Indeed, under the Roman empire, they built cities as we do to-day, all at once, by combining their capital and organising their labour.

The mansion of the Préfet, which is nearly finished, will cost ten millions. The streets are broader than ours in Paris; their difference of level, the elevation of the hills over which they pass, the great spreading plane-trees, of which there are four rows in twenty avenues, the streams of clear water flowing on all sides, and, above all, the enormous harbour, which is being doubled and trebled in size, and the vast structures connected with it, all make of Marseilles a Liverpool of the south.

On my first evening here, after dinner, with a clear sky and good weather, the impression which it made on me was profound. It is a pagan city of the decadence, like Alexandria, Antioch, Rome or Carthage. Immense is the power of a great administrative body, which moves enormous stones, builds palaces, covers them with sculpture, diverts rivers, does everything magnificently; controls the shops, the lights, the great gilded cafés, the theatres, ships, merchandise, warehouses crammed with treasure from all parts of the world.

And not a spark of soul. Nothing but a quest of crude, material, sordid pleasure. There are the lorettes, the girls who dance, the women who sing coarse and catchy songs in the music-halls, the street-walkers, insolent and gaudy, jocular and shallow-pated, caring for nothing but physical pleasure, swaggering luxury, and passing whims—all kept within their grooves by force and custom, by fear of the police and the social organisation. Such towns as this are necessary.

Marseilles is a spoiled city; it is full of jobbery

and dishonesty. Fortunes are made in a hurry, and men are not too particular how they make them. A city of this sort is like the Mirès; but it is productive, it makes money, civilises and fertilises. There is a kind of boldness and liberality which can only thrive on hot-beds. It is different from the philosophical rascaldom and adroit trickery such as we have in Paris, in the pages of Balzac, in the columns of our inferior prints. It is a coarser state of things, proper to the braggart of the south country, who can best you in talk, who is noisy, impudent, and narrow-minded. His only superiority to the Parisian is his greater vitality, the inexhaustible redundancy of his fibre.

BERRE.

BERRE is a little town of 1800 souls, on a tongue of low land, amidst the salt works of the great salt marsh. This great marsh is nine leagues broad, but it is not a lake so much as a lagoon.

There are a few fine old trees, with ample foliage, one of them being as large in girth as six men. A spring, feeding a stream on the southern side, creates a fertile strip of land. But the rest is desolate, and as much neglected as the worst sample of Italy.

Most of the streets are remarkably narrow and evil-smelling, being as dirty as though the dust and mud had been left untouched for centuries. They are rough, with pointed little stones, scattered with refuse, rotten fruit, and vegetables. There are swarms of flies, whose bites inflame the skin. Some of the hovels had their doors open, with a torn curtain hanging across. I could see a mattress, a sleeping man, a woman, and a heap of onions, the whole lighted up by a dazzling sunbeam. Beside a cart laden with grapes were some children, dirty and ragged as lazzaroni, one of them blotched all over his face, others scrofulous, and all were working their fingers into the baskets. Seated on the trunk of a tree was a woman, nursing in her lap a little yellow-faced, black-eyed girl of ten, who was anything but a cleanly object.

The chief hotel is on the strand. It is a big, dilapidated, eighteenth-century barrack of a place, half-deserted, and unclean as a Spanish posada; the ironwork of the front flight of steps has been twisted until the brick steps themselves are disjointed; within, it is like an impromptu picnic. Here, as elsewhere in the neighbourhood, the spirit of lazzaronism prevails.

In the Gard and the Ardèche, I was told by a commercial traveller, the people live on their mulberries and silkworms, which involve about forty days' work in the year. Just now there is a disease amongst the worms, and the mulberries are beginning to disappear. The good folk are none the less merry for that; they chatter, laugh, sit in the cafés, pay three sous for a meal, or even one, though the ordinary price is ten, and spend half the day in idle gossip. Living is wonderfully cheap. A litre of wine, unmixed and heady, costs two sous; a month hence it will only fetch one. They told me of a vinegrower who got rid of his surplus, after a good harvest, by letting the soldiers drink as much as they liked at two sous an hour. Another, being in a hurry for his hogsheads, and not wishing to empty them into the gutter, planted one by the roadside where the soldiers were wont to pass. There was a tap and a glass, and all who cared for it could drink. At Toulouse, a lieutenant told me a similar story. He was taking some recruits through this district, and they were offered wine at one sou the litre.

The grapes are delicious, and the people get them for the trouble of gathering. At Toulouse they pay one sou to enter the vineyards, and the grapes sell for three half-sous in the town.

It is so hot that one needs no more clothing than in Italy. Nature is too kind here; the less we do, the more she indulges us. But humanity gains her positive triumphs in proportion to her physical efforts. If you would leap a ten-foot ditch, you make a twelve-foot spring.

This wine does not keep; it will scarcely bear carrying. They do not make it well; they allow the grapes to become over-ripe, and are not careful enough in cleaning the vats and barrels.

I had a talk with the boatman who rowed me on the lake, and who in the meantime ate grapes, and drank from a large flask of wine. He had seen service in various cruisers, had been to London, to Mexico, Ceylon, and Batavia. On his discharge, he married at forty, and now he has a child, an old sailing-boat, a carrying business between Berre and Martigues; and he does a little fishing. In two years he will be fifty, and will have a pension of twenty-two sous a day; but three per cent. of his wages have been deducted for this since he was fifteen.

It is strange to see how far Socialism has already progressed in France. The State compels you to save money, makes you combine in benefit schemes, whether you like it or not, gives you an allowance when you are sick, and treats you like a child incapable of providing against old age. This guardianship over a nation in its minority greets you at every step. The provinces are like a second France, under the guardianship of Paris, which civilises and emancipates it from a distance by its agents, its movable garrisons, its colonies of officials, its newspapers, and, to some small extent, by its books.

The marsh, which looks blue as a periwinkle before you come close to it, in its bowl of marble, blackened here and there by the weather, is very different when you are sailing over it. The general effect is that of a slaty tint of clouded grey; a sort of dull blue, dimly flecked as it were with wine-lees.

The mountains have little grandeur or character; the impression is simply that of a wide stretch of water under a roof of heavy clouds. There are no waves, nor foam, only the endless agitation, as far as the eye can reach, without effort and without violence, of myriads of little ripples, confined to a sad and commonplace existence.

Berre lies behind us, with its dull red and yellow houses, crowded round the old grey church tower. The bank is so low that they seem to be rising out of the water, and their bold outline stands up from the dubious margin of the marsh. On the northern side the heaps of salt obtrude their harsh white geometrical forms, contrasting with patches of dingy verdure, and the glitter of the silent pools; whilst all around is the starred and creviced basin of the hills, scarred old rocks which seem to have been alternately slashed with a knife and crusted over with lichens.

The lake is in some places as much as thirty feet deep, but large tracts are barely covered with water; and here the submarine growth is of a faint bluish green—thin bare stalks, and a sort of amphibious moss, in which the crabs are interlaced, and the mussels glue themselves together. Other plants raise their tiny heads above the surface, and make a ragged picture to the eye, which has grown accustomed to the bright fluent softness of the wide expanse of waters.

As the wind falls, this monotonous brightness becomes more marked; the ripples sink to rest, and no longer catch the long rays of light; only now an endless succession of luminous waves pierce the deeper shadows, with sparkling pearly tints, then melt into the grey and brown, ever the same, with no sharp line to break the boundless flood of animated light. It might have been a sheet of ice, which swayed without cracking, and by its gentle motion alternately lightened and darkened its melting greens and blacks and greys of light and shade. Meanwhile the sun, high above our heads, darts an infinitude of rays into this great boiling cauldron; and wrapped in this briny mist one sinks into a feverish disquieting torpor.

ORANGE.

THIS is an ugly little hole, with narrow, uneven, dirty streets. And there is a statue of the second Count Raimbaud, who died in the Holy Land, in an odour of sentimental piety, given by Louis Philippe of all men! Here, if anywhere, you appreciate our French centralisation, and its absurd lack of harmony.

But the theatre is unique, and one should not miss seeing it. Here it is plain that we have evidence of a complete civilisation. I could make a study of Sophocles, taking this as my point of departure.

Observe, in the first place, the vast size of the theatre; it would hold fifteen or sixteen thousand persons. The edifice, with its stage and surrounding premises, has a height of thirty-four or thirty-six metres. It is a prodigious structure, reddened and crannied by time, built of blocks as big as the body of a man. Fronting it, against the mountain-side, which saved the necessity of foundations, and formed a natural amphitheatre, are the circular stages of seats, all but the first five rows being now covered with earth, though the shape of the rising tiers is still visible. There are three rows of columns, one above another, and at the top of all is a very high wall, with the well-preserved niches which carried the beams of the upper gallery.

The keeper is an old man of seventy-five, and he has been here since he was twelve. He saw the theatre cleared under Charles X., by M. Caristie, of its hovels, and its three hundred and eighty inhabitants. From the position of the stage, he recited some verses on the ruins, written by Legouvé and Chênedollé, and I heard them from the upper tier as distinctly as if I had been at the Théâtre Français. This gives one a good idea of the declamation of the ancient drama. With the resonant mouthpiece through which they used to speak, the actors must have been easily heard. The arrangement is perfect; the lofty wall at the back throws out the voice with extraordinary clearness.

Here we have the natural outcome of a native southern civilisation in conformity with the climate. Our civilisation of to-day comes from the North, and belongs not so much to citizens as to hard-working, fully-dressed men, who want plays every evening to amuse them, because they are busy all day, and demand a realistic drama, because they are positive and wide-awake. This kind of drama, which is very good for Paris, is an incongruity at Arles and Orange. The genuine drama of the South is such as one would get here, in the open air, under the splendour of the sky, designed for people who loved to sit out in the shady amphitheatres, who lounged and slept on these stone seats, and who, by their bent for expansion and exaggeration, took kindly to the swelling periods of tragic declamation.

A few green fig-trees, dotted with violet figs, a few pomegranates and low shrubs, are scattered about the ruins. A line of broken capitals and shafts of marble show the outer edge of the stage. Everything looks as if it had been pounded. In a niche of the enormous wall is a little ornamental column; at intervals are the attachments of what may have been a marble peristyle; and there are two or three finely worked roses. Nothing has endured save what was held in the indestructible grasp of the heavy stonework.

Looking from the central fig-tree towards the East, one can see the gaping triple series of crumbling vaults. The bright blue sky is cut and torn by their curves or rough edges, a shaky and disjointed framework, tufted with withered plants and dry grasses. More to the right is a lofty fragment of the outer side wall, standing out sheer and without support against the glowing sapphire of the sky. More lofty still the saddle of the mountain rises, grey and tawny; whilst the shapeless ruins are surmounted by all that is left of the castle of the Counts of Orange. They had utilised this theatre as a bastion of their fortress.

The effect is magnificent; it is a victor's prey and trophy. The pile is as grand and picturesque as any of the finest ruins of Italy. Words fail me to convey the impression of those rising tiers, reduced to a shapeless fragment; of those displaced blocks through which the daylight creeps; of those enormous stones, seamed and crannied, with edges chipped and corners broken, eaten away, and ready to fall, whilst some of them are out of their perpendicular, and worn down to their last remaining layer.

LYONS.

I HAVE lounged all day in Lyons, breathing its soft, moist, yet somewhat chilly air. It offers a wonderful contrast to Marseilles.

After several generations in an altered climate, after forming new habits, which become hereditary, a visible change passes over the whole constitution and working of the human machine. On the seacoast of Provence there is no escaping from the hot sun which roasts you like a fire; the heavy choking heat, full of electricity, which oppresses the lungs; the strong mistral, the keen southern wind, which irritates the nerves, dries up the skin, and hurts the eyes; the bare, dry rock, the blue ocean-mirror, beautiful as a violet; the clear horizons, lilac-hued or glowing white. By constant habit a man accommodates himself to his surroundings, and his muscles are braced; he displays more power of resistance, and is tempered to bear extremes; he grows accustomed to sharper contrasts. At the same time he is more excitable, his force of expansion is more prompt and vehement, his accent is sharper and more sonorous, more akin to the note of a horn or a hautboy. And thus he comes to depend more on what is outside of him; he is less self-centred, more drawn to externals, to form, sound, extravagance, outward show, strong sensuous indulgence. But set the same man in a moist temperate peaceful atmosphere, and you will attenuate him, tone him down, and rob him of his keen perceptions.

All variations of climate, soil, and surroundings have their counterpart in the moral domain. There are two reasons which account for this fact, of which the first is to be found in the Darwinian law of selection. Individuals survive the longest, flourish, and reproduce themselves, when they are best fitted for the land they live in. A Fleming in Morocco will be more depressed, less likely to find a suitable mate, and more apt to die, than a Moor. The second reason is the familiar law of adaptation to circumstances, which seems to be virtually at one with that of Darwin. A man gradually and of necessity selects such gestures, attitudes, ideas, and actions, habits, instincts, and aptitudes as are most in accord with his surroundings, the rest being little by little effaced by weariness and pain—that is, by incompatibility.

Physiologists tell us that the stomach, the lungs,

the skin, every organ and every molecule, is associated with all the rest. Therefore each organ varies in condition as the body varies in its action, so that by the law of persistency of type, the tendency to continue the condition which is most frequent, there is a tendency to reproduce the physiological condition most harmonious with a particular system of actions—which explains the accommodation of mood in the individual.

CROSSING THE JURA.

ANOTHER soil, another sky, another world! The roofs grow steeper, and fall halfway across the wings, in order to protect the walls against the oblique rains. The whole house bristles with its armour of dark red tiles, fit colour for an armed man. All around is green—plains and hillsides, winding roads, the very crests of the mountains, with a dull soaked green, eternally drenched by the rolling mists. It is impossible to describe the force of the contrast for one who has just left the white bare mountains of the South. They have not a hue in common. The green of the meadows becomes delicate and soft, from the pale yellow of the early growths of spring to a delightful but transitory brilliance, like the blossom of a flower. All the earth tints are strong, the houses white and red, the roofs blackened, the fir plantations dark. Yet the sky, heavy with rain-clouds, is brown or muddy-yellow. The fogs hang in the distance like soaked tiles, the near ones float in the evening like motionless gauze. The constantly-watered grass looks as if it would never wither. Here and there is a sleepy river, with long bright sheets of water, quiet and almost black, like the surface of a marsh, which reflects the sky as in a mirror. Even the face and form of humanity has changed; the people are taller, less lively, less cheerful and familiar. The universal greenness and moisture, the firs and the mountains, breed a sadder and more serious idea of life. One shudders slightly at the thought of winter, prepares oneself against it, and adds to the comforts of one's house.

STRASBOURG.

The interior of the Cathedral is the finest example of Gothic which I have seen.

As you enter, it is like night. There is not a single transparent window; all are coloured and dark. And there are windows everywhere—on your right and on your left, and in both the high galleries. A strange light, a sort of purple shadow, pervades the vast nave. There are no seats here; only five or six kneeling worshippers, or silent wandering shades. We are rid for a time of our paltry little houses, of the paltry insect-life of humanity. The broad space between the pillars is bare to the vaulted roof, occupied only by dubious lights and a vast, almost palpable shade.

In front of us the choir is exceptionally dark; one window stands out brightly from the centre of the apse, filled with shining figures, like a vista of Paradise. The choir, nevertheless, is crowded with priests; but the darkness is so deep, and the distance so great, that there is nothing to be seen. There are no visible decorations or little objects of worship; only two chandeliers sparkle in the gloom with lighted tapers, like tremulous souls, at the two corners of the altar, amidst the grand carvings which one is merely permitted to imagine. The antiphons rise and fall at regular intervals, like a swinging censer; sometimes the clear far-off voices of the choir make one think that one hears the singing of cherubim; now and again the organ swells out above every other sound with majestic harmony.

I went up to the entrance of the choir, and from thence the oriental rose-window, more severe and noble than in any other cathedral, shone forth above the vast obscurity of the nearer arches, in its framing of blue and black. The colossal pillars came into view; the deep shadows and the splendid contrast of the dim light were like an image of the Christian life immersed in this gloomy world, with its rare outlets into the next. On both sides, as far as the eye could penetrate into the dome, the whole sacred narrative was blazoned on the glass in violet and red, like a revelation vouchsafed to poor humanity.

How well the men of old understood the effect of light and shade! This Cathedral speaks to the eyes at once, and in its entirety. What place has argument here? The symbol conveys everything, and makes everything understood. Words cannot paint this vast avenue of stone, with its solemn pillars in regular courses, never weary under the burden of that sublime vault. It is a world, an abstract of the great world—to grope from place to place, to feel your way against the chilly walls, in a life of gloom, amidst the doubtful tremulous light, the feeble muttering and whispering of the human swarm, and for consolation to catch a hagioscope of radiant figures far above you, a canopy of azure, the divine eyes of a Virgin and Child, of a Christ with His hands outstretched in benediction, whilst grand psalms, high notes well sustained, a concert of jubilant acclamation, lift the soul to Heaven upon their undulations of harmony.

Amongst other fine details is the ancient arching of the vaults in the crypt and choir. This is a solid effect, and in fact Roman; it is the nucleus and centre around which the Gothic has blossomed luxuriantly.

In a chapel on the northern side, almost dark and rarely used, is a large recumbent stone figure of Bishop Conrad of Lichtemberg, the founder, who died in 1299. He lies on his tomb, with a book in his hand. He looks like a Pharaoh, who has slept from all eternity. The pulpit, which is not large, dates from 1486, and is a marvel of delicacy, with foliage, heads, interlacing designs, and nearly fifty statues. The Gothic in its final phase develops into a gem.

I returned again and again to the choir and apse, to their round columns, their grand massive circle, strong and sombre, to the ancient Roman Christianity, the planted shoot which has become great and indestructible, and around which all the rest has broken into bloom.

I do not altogether care for the church outside. The towers are massive, and, in order to lighten them, they have been decked with a cloak, a network of decoration, a filigree of statues and fine mouldings. There is only one clock-tower, so that the edifice appears to have lost a limb; no one seems to have thought that it needed a corresponding tower on the other side. The one which is here already is a rich efflorescence, quite artificial in style; the stonework has been laid on to an iron frame. It aptly illustrates the character of this exaggerated art, which had not the common sense to insist on order and symmetry, such as might develop into bloom later on. Many Gothic Cathedrals have their towers quite detached, at a distance of fifty paces. This particular civilisation is all on the same plan —a grand, vehement, sometimes delicate fancy, but still the fancy of a sick man.

The statues are admirable. Here, no doubt, is an art like that which, almost at the same time, produced a Van Eyck in Flanders. Erwin of Heinbach died in 1318; the northern tower was finished in 1365; the spire was completed in 1439.

I was charmed to find a dawn of art in these statues. These men had left behind them the monastic feebleness of the Middle Age, the hieratic childishness of the sculptures of Chartres, which made the heads stupid, and a quarter of the length of the body. They had a notion of proportion, they were masters of their craft, and for the first time they present us with a man. They catch at once, with energy, with the freshness and delight of inventors, the full expression of an attitude, the hang of a cloak, a typical head, a movement of the body. How fortunate that they did not copy, but invented! There is not one adopted type; they had actualities before their eyes, and drew thence every variety of the human face and attitude.

Look at the strange mischievous smile, full of covetous menace, on the face of one of the Foolish Virgins; at the goodness, perhaps a little heavy and constitutional, in the square head of a Wise Virgin. Some of these artists were really of the first rank, though full of realism. They found an ideal, not the only ideal, nor yet after the antique model, but in accord with the fresh delight of their eyes and of their heart.

In the middle porch is an Eve, undraped. She is

T

a German woman, somewhat fleshy, just a trifle sulky, too closely copied for our taste from the actual nude, but full-blooded, and sure to produce fine children. The Apostles are austere, lean, with long faces, pensive and energetic, dressed with dignity, abounding in force; and their attitude is as though taken from the life.

On the middle front are two female statues, the Church and the Synagogue, which are attributed to Sabina, the daughter of Erwin. They are very fine and bear testimony to a complete as well as a new art. The heads are noble and full of thought, with long and beautiful hair falling somewhat thickly; the figures are slim and supple, well set off by the delicately folded robes. It may be that a whole life of thought and meditation was devoted to the conception of these types. This is the happiness of the artist; when he works, and is endowed with genius, he comes at last to see his heart's innermost ideal revealed to him alone, taking form before him, and to bestow upon it an actual embodiment. What bliss, at such a moment, to discover that a supple figure, a delicate head surmounted by its flowing hair, reveals a pure and lofty soul!

On the northern front is a porch, erected in 1494, most richly carved, with festoons of briar, waving branches, twining knots — another gem of the decadence. But the eight carved figures, including an armed knight, a courtier, and, finest of all, a crowned Virgin (German again), with a diadem of magnificent locks, wrapped in contemplation, and bearing her child in her arms, display once more the birth of a new and grand art.

Sculpture succeeds architecture, and man succeeds the Deity, as the State replaces the Church, and the modern age follows upon the mediæval.

What a keen, a chaste, a bold perception of the individual, the distinct type! The courtier with his high cheek-bones, slender legs, stern and prominent eyes; the old and simple knight, weary after long endurance, and heroic to the last, are speaking portraitures.

I had some conversation with Mlle. Jeanne C——, who is at a convent school in Strasbourg, a branch of the *Oiseaux*. She is thirteen, a flower in the bud, slender and tall. And she looked like a bird, as she sat at table in the evening, silent, with downcast eyes, elegant and slim in her pretty dress. It was the strange charm of maidenhood, of the unsophisticated soul, the mind too timid to reveal itself, with all the world before it. Next morning, after a five hours' ride, she unbent, and prattled. She was a girl and a boy in one. You have there the inception and the collapse of illusion.

Her school is such a good one that she is rejoicing over the completion of her holidays. The sisters are all like mothers; they are addressed as " Ma mère," and the Superior as " Maman." They punish very little, and then it is a grief to all of them. The worst infliction is to be deprived of their belt, for every class has its belt—red, yellow, blue, or white. Once there was a terrible punishment. The offence was so serious that nobody ever knew what it was. The guilty one had to wear an old dress and cap all the day long, both in class and at meals. They are never locked up or deprived of dainties; and the food is very good.

They play with the utmost spirit and enthusiasm, tossing the ball or racing, and they shout like children and madcaps. A great point is made of it, and those who will not play have bad marks.

Each girl has her favourite sister, who is her intimate friend. She tells her everything, kisses her, and conceals nothing from her adopted mother. The sisters, having no other object in life, no ambition, no desire to be in better circumstances, no vanity, no prospect of marriage and children, throw their whole heart into this life. The girls come and see them in after years, for they are friends never to be forgotten.

They pay six hundred francs a year. There are fifty boarders, with thirty-two lay-sisters, and others;

and there is room for two hundred and fifty. The establishment was re-founded two years ago by ladies who came from the *Oiseaux;* and the numbers are steadily increasing.

It is clear that the secular establishments cannot stand against a competition of this kind. The only objections to convent schools are that the life is made too pleasant; the children are spoiled both for ordinary existence and for marriage; the teaching is too poor, for the pupils have no stimulus and no constraint, merely taking up what they please. It is the same with the religious establishments for boys; when it rains on Sunday they have a half-holiday on the first fine day. Again, if a girl is rich and imaginative, she is often lured into taking the veil. I have heard of several instances.

It is a special characteristic of the Church in France that it is a temporal institution and a machinery of government. The religious sentiment properly so called, the moral, mystic, artistic feeling, such as one sees in Germany, in Italy, and in England, is almost non-existent, and at best spasmodic or rudimentary. The main thing is the feeling of docility, the necessity of conforming to certain rules and acquiring certain habits, an acquiescence of the reason in the working of a beautiful machinery and a regular organisation, with unity in the sense that Bossuet enjoined. In short, the Church is a powerful, well-disciplined body, which finds places for its members, and which exacts obedience from them.

At a tavern in the Vosges I was reading a report of Monseigneur de Ségur on the progress of a certain association. The priests make a point of having had so many communicants at Easter, on such and such a day. The assistants all send up reports and figures, and they are promoted according to the number of their conquests. The prevailing spirit is that of acquisition and domination.

Are we still Gauls, with Druids not to be extirpated, with a nineteenth-century Vercingetorix, and our administrative hierarchy imported by Rome?

Our most conspicuous defect in any kind of action is the want of leaders and guides. Most of the people I come across make a poor show, or do nothing at all, for want of guidance; a very small minority, say one in a thousand, have general and independent ideas. Professors, retired officials, archæologists, and men in the army, whom I visit on my yearly rounds, are wont to lounge about, pass their time at the café, sleep in their armchairs, or collect curiosities. They have no aim or object.

To-day I drove to Sainte Odile.

It is a convent, showing the remains of a Roman

crypt, and was founded in the eighth century on the side of a mountain.

The day was magnificent. We drove for three hours through a forest of pines and fir-trees. For the first half-hour the effect was admirable. The trees are tall and strong, and in vigorous growth. I am never weary of looking at these straight, superbly-soaring, splendidly-shaped trunks, like a phalanx of young heroic savages. The firs, with their smooth bark, variegated by light-coloured moss, are more beautiful than the pines; their branches are of a fresher and more vivid green. They are massed together in groups, and their silvery bark cuts clear into the azure sky. You will see two or three on a slope, standing alone, motionless, like an advanced post on an enemy's frontier, in all the pride and beauty of youth. Others descend into the valley, like an army on the march. Their dense rings of foliage blot out the sun; only through the colonnades of the trunks can you get sight of it, dimmed and transfigured as you may see it through the blazoned panes of a cathedral. Elsewhere, in a clearing, it pours down upon you with startling suddenness, with magnificent splendour, and streams in a sheet of light over the moss, over the shining screen of lichens, over the long drooping branches. And down beneath this flood of sunshine you can discern in the silent shadow the slender forms of myriads of young fir-trees, delicately soaring up like the pillars in a Gothic fane.

But the most admirable sight of all is that of the setting sun, from the summit of Sainte Odile. Every hill is wooded to the top. There is a never-ending succession of trees, as far as the eye can reach, swarming up into the sky, a dark border instinct with life. Yet here and there a patch of meadow, as large as your hand, sparkles with a brighter green. Nothing but trees in endless procession, in incredible numbers, an infinite array, swarming wherever you may look, undisturbed in their ancient and peaceful domain. They gather in squadrons upon the rounded crests, descend the slopes, concentrate in the valleys, and climb again to the sharper summits of the central mountain. The whole vast army advances in mighty waves from crest to crest, like some barbarian host, shrouded in gloom and not to be numbered.

Above them, a sky of inimitable blue rings them round, with wondrous joy and serenity. The sun sheds his golden light on the battalions in the van, whilst the rear is enfolded in a luminous mist; and away to the east a fair wide plain, clearly distinguished by its softer hues, presents a rich booty of cultivated fields to that wild invading host of trees.

THE END.

syx

14 DAY USE
RETURN TO DESK FROM WHICH BORROWED
LOAN DEPT.

This book is due on the last date stamped below, or on the date to which renewed.
Renewed books are subject to immediate recall.

---

31 Aug'64 WC

~~SANTA BARBARA~~
INTERLIBRARY LOAN

THREE WEEKS   FLDT

REC'D LD NON-RENEWABLE
          3-28-72
SEP 14 '64 -12 M   0338

13 Oct '64 RR   MAR 2   1972

REC'D LD

JAN 30 '65 -3 PM

13 Feb

REC'D LD

JUN 10 '65 -2 PM

LD 21A–60m-4,'64
(E4555s10)476B

General Library
University of California
Berkeley

302446

UNIVERSITY OF CALIFORNIA LIBRARY

www.ingramcontent.com/pod-product-compliance
Lightning Source LLC
Chambersburg PA
CBHW030014240426
43672CB00007B/951